Robert Taylor Pritchett

Pen and Pencil Sketches of Shipping and Craft all Round the World

Robert Taylor Pritchett
Pen and Pencil Sketches of Shipping and Craft all Round the World
ISBN/EAN: 9783337190569
Printed in Europe, USA, Canada, Australia, Japan
Cover: Foto ©ninafisch / pixelio.de

More available books at **www.hansebooks.com**

PEN AND PENCIL SKETCHES

OF

SHIPPING AND CRAFT

ALL ROUND THE WORLD

BY

R. T. PRITCHETT

Marine Painter to the Royal Thames Yacht Club

LONDON
EDWARD ARNOLD
Publisher to the India Office
37, BEDFORD STREET, STRAND
1899

DEDICATED

TO THE RIGHT HON.

THE LORD BRASSEY, K.C.B.

IN PLEASANT RECOLLECTION OF MANY THOUSAND

MILES IN THE "SUNBEAM," R.Y.S.

BY HIS GRATEFUL LIMNER

R. T. PRITCHETT.

INTRODUCTION.

THE Victorian period of the present century is characterised by rapid evolution. The Red Indian is rapidly falling back before the white man and the march of intellect. The brown fibre and mat sails of the craft in savage countries are being supplanted by our well-beloved white canvas, and already is our faithful old servant the picturesque canvas driven out by the more powerful yet controllable motor "steam." Even the snow-white sails of our beautiful "Britannias," "Ailsas," and "Valkyries" have to give way to pole-master steam yachts, in spite of the misery of the dreadful coaling.

How much we owe to canvas! How well it served our early discoverers in their little ships, those pioneers of England's future glory on the high seas, Columbus, Magellan, Drake, Frobisher, Cook, Anson!

The canvas period was a grand period in England's history, recalling glorious deeds of courage, daring, and patriotism, when our navy was opening up the great highway for the development of commerce. What associations were recalled when the British fleet sailed for the Russian waters! What a grand sight were the 50-gun frigates or 120-gun line-of-battle ships under a crowd of canvas, every stitch set and drawing, with wide-spreading studding sails on both sides; or the noble teak-built East Indiaman in full sail, or a China tea clipper cracking on in the Trades. These are now bygones, and replaced by wonders of modern science, such as our Atlantic greyhounds the "Campania" or the steamers of the "Orient" line; to say nothing of those features of this age, our grim signal-masted ironclads or torpedo destroyers, of which the British Navy is now composed, and of which every Englishman must be proud.

The opening of the Suez Canal tolled the knell of parting canvas and opened the back-door of Eastern Europe to receive the rich products of India and China direct, instead of coming by long sea voyages in the stately ships of our merchant princes round the Cape of Good Hope, or in our celebrated China tea clippers, which were real racers. An instance of rapid and accelerated communication is shown by the fact that a letter posted at Peshawur, North India, January 26th, arrived in due course at London on February 10th—steam *per mare et terras*.

Again, rounding Cape Horn, the most southern point of South America, against "the brave westerlies," was a trying time for sailing ships, sometimes for weeks in snow- and hail-storms and gales of wind. Steamers now avoid this by running through the Straits of Magellan to the west coast of South America, Chili, and Peru, only to find that the steam-horse on land has cut them out by a short overland route from Buenos Ayres on the east coast.

Long voyages in the "Wanderer," R.Y.S., and "Sunbeam," R.Y.S., under the white ensign, afforded me great opportunities of seeing fibre and mat-sailed craft in the Far East, the Malay Archipelago, and South Seas, and of delighting in the balloon canvas in the Trades, whilst the auxiliary steam was a luxury when wanted in flat calms in mid-ocean or entering narrow harbours. Some of the subjects have been considered interesting enough to be brought together to form the present volume, accompanied by short descriptions, making "Pen and Pencil Sketches of Shipping and Craft all round the World," commencing with the Royal yacht "Victoria and Albert," and ending with Malay proas at the Murray Islands in the Antipodes.

R. T. PRITCHETT.

CONTENTS

		PAGE
KINA BATANGAN RIVER-BOAT		*Frontispiece*
"VICTORIA AND ALBERT" .	England .	2
"BRITANNIA" .	,,	6
"SUNBEAM," R.Y.S. .	,,	10
CHINA TEA CLIPPER . . .	,,	14
COLLIER, COAL-WHIPPING IN THE THAMES	,,	18
YORKSHIRE COBLES . .	,,	22
A MEDWAY BARGE	,,	26
MANX AND PENZANCE FISHING BOATS AND BRIXHAM TRAWLER . .		30
THE "CORK" LIGHTSHIP AND TURBINE LIFEBOAT OFF HARWICH . .	,,	34
ICE BOATS ON THE HUDSON AND AT ST. MORITZ		38
THE AMERICA CUP. THE "VIGILANT" WINNING FROM THE "VALKYRIE" .	United States	42
"GOVERNOR AMES," FIVE-MASTED TRADING SCHOONER . . .	,,	46
A GUNDALOW AND A MAINE PINKEY	,,	50
THE BERMUDA RIG . . .	Bermuda	54
SYDNEY FLYING SQUADRON .	Australia	58
NORWEGIAN JAEGT AND FISHING-BOAT	Norway	62
NORWEGIAN HERRING BOATS .	,,	66
DANISH COASTER AT ROSKILDE	Denmark	70
ZOUT WATER SCHIP; FLUSHING .	Holland	74
SCHEVENINGEN; DUTCH "PINK" COMING IN		78

		PAGE
HELIGOLAND BOAT	Heligoland	82
BLANKENBURG BRIG	Belgium	86
CHASSE-MARÉE	France	90
A "MOLETA" FISHING BOAT	Portugal	94
SPANISH COASTER OFF CAPE VILLANO	Spain	98
ALGERINE CRAFT; COAST OF BARBARY	Barbary	102
VENETIAN FISHING-BOATS AT BERGOZZI	Italy	106
SMYRNA CRAFT	Turkey and Egypt	110
A CONSTANTINOPLE CAIQUE	,,	114
THE KHEDIVE'S DAHABEAH	,,	118
A NILE NUGGER	,,	122
A NILE GYASSI	,,	126
ARAB DHOWS	Indian Ocean	130
A PIRATE OF THE PERSIAN GULF	,,	134
LATEEN RACERS, ROYAL BOMBAY YACHT CLUB	India and Ceylon	138
OUTRIGGER FISHING-BOATS, COLOMBO	,,	142
COLOMBO COASTER	,,	146
RICE BOAT ON THE IRRAWADDY RIVER	Burmah	150
RIVER BOATS, RANGOON	,,	154
SAMPANS AT MOULMEIN	,,	158
TIEN-SIEN JUNKS	Singapore	162
A KOLEH	,,	166
PEKALONGAN FISHING BOAT	Java	170
PROBOLINGO FISHING BOAT	,,	174
MACASSAR CRAFT	Celebes	178
PIRATE CRAFT OFF NORTH POINT OF BORNEO	Borneo	182
SULU CRAFT OFF SANDAKAU	,,	186
CHINESE PIRATE JUNK	China	190
JAPANESE FISHING BOATS	Japan	194
BAHIA RIVER CRAFT	Brazil	198
THE "BOLSA" OR SKIN-BOAT	Chili	202
THE LEAUKA, FIJI	Fiji	206
A CANOE OF THE ABORIGINES	The Antipodes	210

SHIPPING AND CRAFT.

ENGLAND.

THE ROYAL YACHTS.
"*VICTORIA AND ALBERT.*"

THE national pastime of yachting certainly deserves to take precedence of most craft-history in matters maritime in British waters. Of the Royal Yacht Squadron her Majesty the Queen has been the patroness ever since 1837, presenting annually a hundred guinea cup to be sailed for, members only. Immediately after the war in 1815, the numerous large yachts then in existence and frequenting Cowes were brought together by their enthusiastic owners, and a club was organised at Cowes by the most influential men of the day, and firmly established, with royal patronage and wealth to back it. Cowes in fact has been the one great centre of attraction, where, during the first week in August every year, the finest yachts and cruisers are concentrated, not only the competing craft, but the Royal Yacht of our own Royal Family, and the craft of other nations also, American, German, and French.

When the Queen succeeded to the throne, the Royal Yacht was a sailing vessel, shiprigged, laid down in Deptford in 1814, from the design of Sir Henry Peake, and launched in July, 1817, as the "Royal George." She came therefore into the service of her fourth Sovereign when Queen Victoria succeeded to the throne. It will be interesting to compare the dimensions of this yacht for State progresses, with those of H.R.H. the Prince of Wales's Racing Cutter the "Britannia," in 1898.

1817.	1898.
THE "ROYAL GEORGE."	"BRITANNIA," R.Y.S.
Full Ship Rig.	Racing Cutter.
Length, 103 ft.	L.O.A., 121·5 ft.
Breadth, 26 ft. 8 in.	L.W.L., 87·8 ft.
Depth of hold, 11 ft. 6 in.	Breadth, 23·66 ft.
Burthen in tons, 330.	Depth, 15 ft.
	151·13 Y.R.A. rating
	(say 300 tons).
	Sail area, 10,328 square feet.

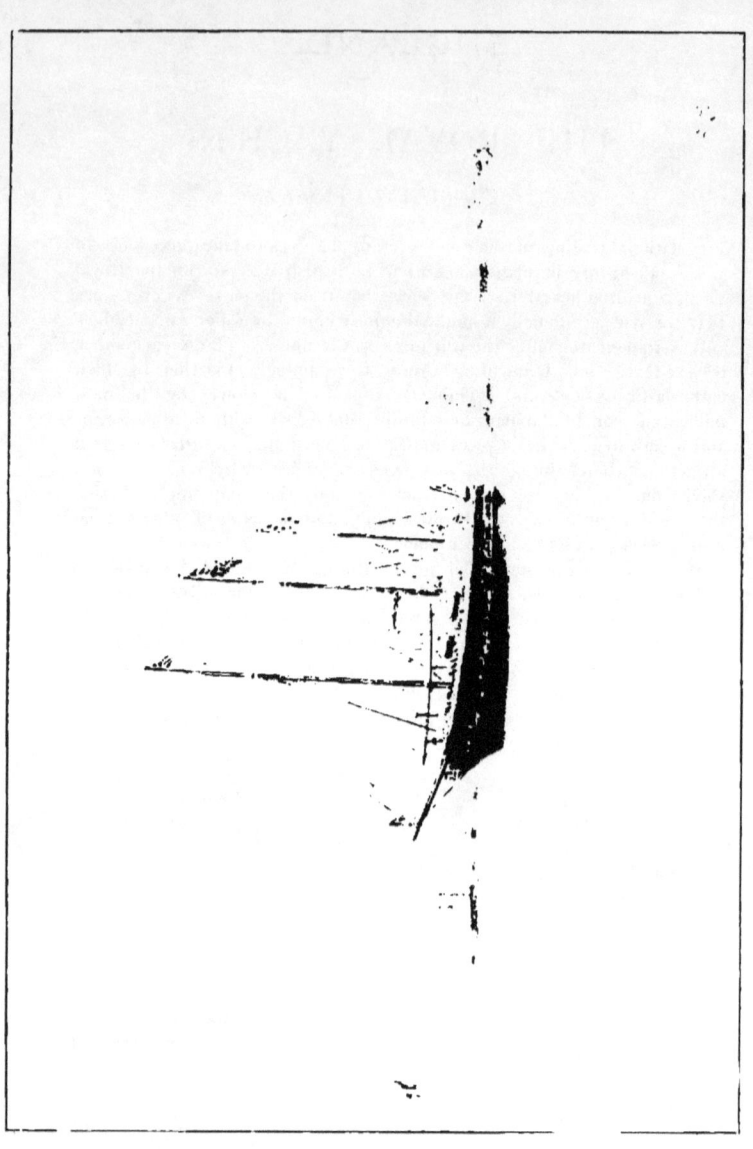

"VICTORIA AND ALBERT."

The Queen's visit to Scotland in 1842 sealed the fate of the "Royal George." The time had come when the uncertainty of canvas had to give way to the certainty of steam. Bad weather necessitated the Royal yacht being taken in tow by H.M. steamer "Shearwater," and the Admiralty yacht "Black Eagle"; her Majesty returning south in the "Trident," a steamship belonging to the General Steam Navigation Company.

From this time the "Royal George" has been laid up in Portsmouth Harbour, and attains this year the good age of eighty-two.

In 1842 a new steam yacht was laid down at Pembroke, November 9th, from the design of Sir William Symonds. Extreme length, 225 ft.; beam, 39 ft.; ditto over paddle boxes, 59 ft.; speed, $11\frac{2}{10}$ knots; commissioned July 1, 1843. This was an early period of steamships; the right combinations had not been worked out; great vibration was produced by too much propelling force. 1855 produced a new "Victoria and Albert," a grand specimen of naval architecture, designed by Oliver Lang, master shipwright of Pembroke Dockyard. Length over all, 336·4 ft.; beam outside paddle boxes, 66·6 ft.; tonnage, 2,342; speed, 16·813 and 17 knots.

But now it is paddle boxes, or "side boxes," that are doomed, and her Majesty's new steam yacht, also built at Pembroke Dockyard, 1899, is up to date with twin screws, forced draught, telephones, and electric appliances; in fact a model of scientific construction and equipment, having a length of 380 ft. between perpendiculars; beam, 50 ft.; displacement, 4,700 tons; H.P. indicated, 11,000.

ENGLAND.

THE ROYAL YACHT SQUADRON.

"*BRITANNIA.*"

The most celebrated yachts of bygone days were certainly the "Pearl," the "Arrow," and the "Alarm." The "Pearl" was a 120-ton cutter, built in 1820 for the Marquis of Anglesey, by Santy the Smuggler who sailed from the Colne, a staunch supporter and prime mover at the foundation of the Royal Yacht Squadron. The "Arrow" was designed by her owner, Joseph Weld, Esq., of Lulworth Castle. She passed into the hands of Thomas Chamberlayne, Esq. The celebrated "Alarm" was built in 1830, also from the design of Joseph Weld. Her tonnage as a cutter, her first rig, was 193 tons. After the visit of the "America" in 1851, Mr. Weld lost no time in profiting thereby, and at once altered the bow of the "Alarm" by 20 ft., and gave her flat canvas, the mainsail and staysail, including jib, both laced to the boom for windward work, in which our visitor excelled.

Coming to present days, we are proud to have amongst all the cracks of the period one vessel whose name will be handed down as the most perfect combination of racing and cruising qualities ever achieved; and what a good name she bears. It was a happy thought to christen her "Britannia," for she well deserves it, representing in many details the best work that has been produced by the designer, the builder, the sailmaker, the skipper, and the crew. Her original owner, H.R.H. the Prince of Wales, by his practical interest in every class of yachting at home and abroad, has developed each phase of the sport; even the small raters have had special patronage. When the Prince gave a £100 cup, in 1898, to be sailed for by these famous little fellows, they sailed in nearly a gale of wind. Of the Solent One class, eighteen started from the R.Y. "Osborne," and gave a grand display of what amateurs can make of bad weather in a splendid race won by "Tangerine."

The "Britannia" was designed by G. L. Watson, and came out in 1893. Every one was anxious for her success, and she proved to be worthy of their confidence and hopes.

Measurements of the "Britannia"—L.O.A., 121·5 ft.; L.W.L., 87·8 ft.; breadth, 23·66 ft.; depth, 15 ft.; rating, 151·13 Y.R.A.; sail area, 10,328 sq. ft. The years 1893 and 1894 soon put her qualities to a severe test, for the American "Navahoe" came over to challenge for the Gold Cup of the Victoria Club. The challenge was taken up by the "Britannia," who won three out of five races and retained the trophy. The illustration shows "Britannia" running up off Ryde with housed topmast, and leading "Navahoe." The latter was a beautiful boat, designed by Herreshoff, and represented a remarkable blend of American lines and the English cutter type. She was, however, very tender, and not up to the weight of our English breezes. She started eighteen times and won five prizes.

In 1893 the "Britannia" won the Queen's Cup at Plymouth, and the Queen's Cup in the Clyde, taking in her first year, in addition to these, twenty-seven prizes. Mr. William Jameson represented the Prince all through her brilliant career, whilst Captain John Carter was her skipper, a proud position to hold.

In 1894 came the tug-of-war for the America Cup. The defender, the "Vigilant," came over after beating "Valkyrie" at Sandy Hook. She was one of Herreshoff's designs, with a centre-board, but her experiences during her visit here tolled the knell of centre-boards for big boats in this country as well as in America. The "Vigilant" met the "Britannia," with the result that she was beaten twelve times in eighteen starts. She was, however, a much more powerful boat than "Navahoe," even with her centre-board down.

The race on the Clyde for the Queen's Cup in 1894 was a scene of extraordinary excitement, and Scotch enthusiasm was at fever heat, the shore black with spectators, and the water crowded with every kind of boat. It was a grand and close race, and the visitor was allowed plenty of room to round her last mark. The "Britannia" won, to the joy of all. The only regret, however, was that the Prince was not there *in propriâ persona*, to see how "Britannia" "kept the goal."

In 1895 the Prince's cutter carried off all three cups given at Cowes, Ryde, and Queenstown; and now the "Britannia," having done credit to all connected with her, stands forth as the grandest all-round cutter of modern times—not as a racing machine, but as a delightful home and wholesome craft in bad weather.

ENGLAND.

THE ROYAL YACHT SQUADRON.

THE "SUNBEAM."

So well known is this yacht that her name is almost a household word, and her doings and cruisings have given pleasure to thousands of people who hardly know what a yacht really is. She claims prominent mention, in that when she first came out she founded a new class and period in yachting.

In 1854 Lord Brassey, then Mr. Brassey, began his experiences with an eight-ton cutter, which gave him a real zest for sailing; and in 1857 he won the Queen's Cup in the Mersey with "Cymba," a 50-ton cutter, designed and built by Fife of Fairlie. From 50 tons the next step was to the "Albatross," then to an auxiliary schooner of 164 tons, the "Meteor," followed by "Muriel," Dan Hatcher's favourite 40-tonner; and the "Eothen" auxiliary, 340 tons. Based on his experience of twenty years, Lord Brassey decided to have an auxiliary steam yacht after his own heart, to the design of Mr. Alexander Richardson. The love acquired in early days with "Cymba" for canvas had to be carefully considered, for the new yacht was not to be a steamboat, but, as a model cruiser, she was to be fast under canvas, with auxiliary steam power only to help her in doldrums or dead calm, or again, when she should be well in command, going into harbours or through narrow passages with a head wind. Time has shown that these qualities were well carried out, as proved by the "Sunbeam's" record of ocean cruising in 1874, 12,747 knots; in 1876-7, one cruise, 37,000 knots round the world; 1883, 13,545 knots in a cruise to the West Indies. And then she started for a second voyage round the world, a voyage cut short by the sad death of the late Lady Brassey, whose travels, and the bright way in which she related them, have delighted many.

Having given some idea of the performance of the "Sunbeam" as a cruiser, let us turn to some of the details of her construction and rig. Material of hull: iron frame with teak skin; built at Liverpool in 1874.

  Length over all.......... 170 ft.   Engines by Laird of Birken-
  Length on water line   150 ft.   head.

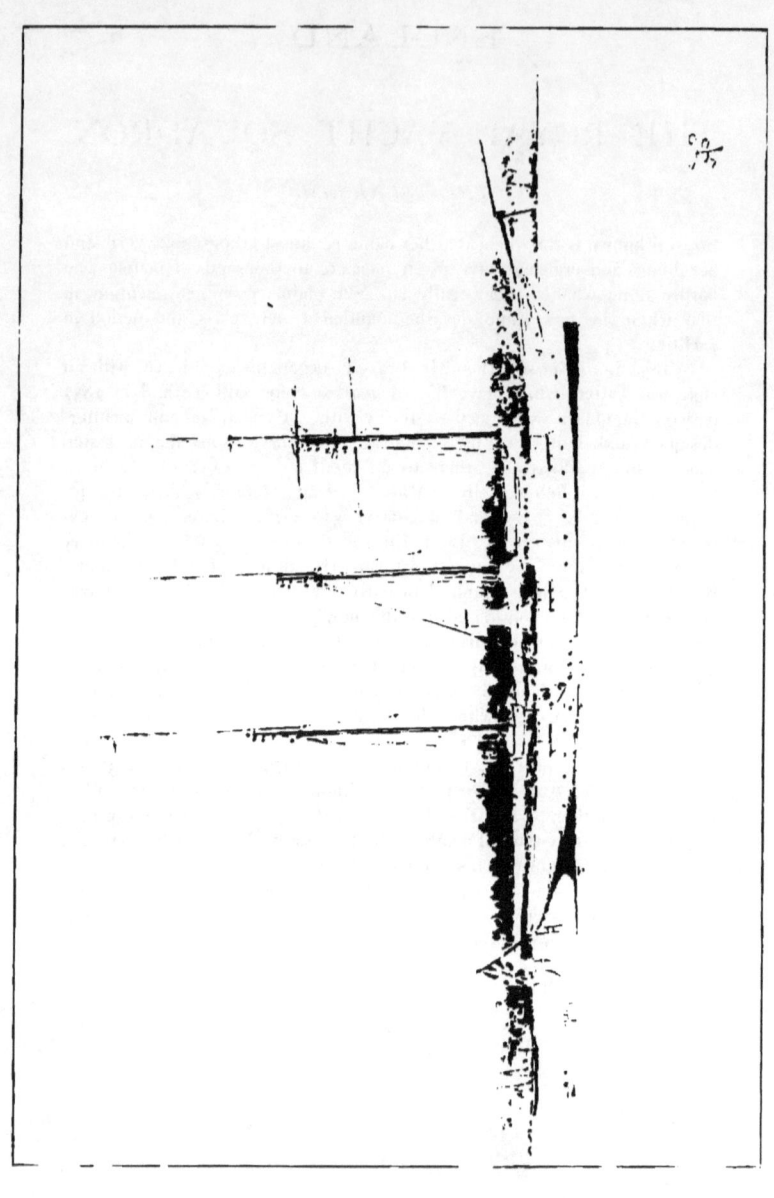

Beam .... 27 ft.	Horse power, 70 nominal
Depth of hold .... 13 ft. 9 in.	indicated, 380.
Tonnage Displacement 576 tons.	Stowage of coal, 70 tons.
Draught .... 13·6 feet.	,, ,, water, 16 tons.
Original sail area ... 9,200 sq. ft.	Lead ballast, 75 tons.

For the trade winds extra balloon canvas.

The success of the combination of good qualities in her led to the "Chazalie" being built in 1875, followed by the "Czarina," for Mr. Albert Brassey, in 1877. Then the "Lancashire Witch" in 1878, which made some wonderfully long runs in ocean cruising. This quartet settled the qualities required, and started auxiliary steam yachts on a firm basis, the "Sunbeam" being the Madre of the fleet.

After this, riches and luxury went for bigger game, and now we have steam yachts of immense size, like private hotels-de-luxe, or palatial mail steamers. In America everything is on a large scale, and Mr. Vanderbilt has a steam yacht, the "Valiant," 2,350 tons, brig-rig; whilst in our own home waters may be seen Mr. Laycock's "Valhalla," 1,400 tons, ship-rigged. It is hard to credit that she is a yacht when bearing down on you, until perchance the white ensign may be seen flying at the peak or the R.Y.S. burgee at the main. Burgees seem rather out of place in these large craft.

For a long cruise there is no doubt that Lord Brassey's "Sunbeam" has been a great success; and the owner has always been her navigator. She is large enough for any weather anywhere, for Lord Brassey's experiences vary from studding sails and skyscrapers to being battened down and laid to, with canvas reduced to one jib headed main trysail.

On one occasion, in the West Indies in 1883, I remember the weather bright and clear, temperature perfect, every stitch that could be carried set, studding sails on both sides and jackyarders. Looking up with admiration from the taffrail, Lord Brassey suggested a trip to the flying jibboom so as to study the "Beauty" from that point of view. We were well rewarded; looking up we saw the clean white canvas splendidly illumined by the bright sun shining through it, the graceful curves of the sail, the tension of the sheets, the rich colour of the spars, and suggestive bend of the studding sail-boom. That was above; below was the grander sight by far, her white hull, ploughing with her fine bow through the deep blue waters of the Spanish main, was beautified by the contrast of her bright copper, the colour of which was graduated from the water-polished surface to the richer tones left from the last visit of the copper punt.

And then, on another occasion, between Cape Hatteras and Bermuda, she laid to in a long gale like a duck, with reefed trysails, although constantly luffed up to meet an unusually big comber.

ENGLAND.

OUR MERCANTILE MARINE.

TEA CLIPPERS.

OUR Mercantile Marine at the commencement of the present reign was magnificent. The Honourable East India Company had created a class of ships which were very properly described in the sailing notices as "Frigate Teak-built East Indiamen." They were grand vessels, and the East India Docks presented a sight worth going miles to see when the proud craft rested in the basin, gathered in under the wing of the old deep redmast-house of Blackwall. In those days Messrs. Green were famous builders; there was also Messrs. Wigram's yard, now converted into a Midland Railway goods terminus. Blackwall, with the Trinity House close by, was a centre of mercantile marine in "the forties."

The business transacted by the merchant princes of the city of London was carried out smoothly, the mail days coming round in their regular course, outward mails and home mails; but the change was coming. The Brazilian mails, which went out in man-of-war brigs from Falmouth to Rio de Janeiro and La Plata, were probably amongst the first to give way and bow to the inevitable. In the early forties the Royal West India Mail Steam Packet Company began to run two fast schooners down to British Guiana in South America. The Great Western Steamship was already running from Bristol to America. That gave an impulse to shipbuilders, who gave up the frigate teak-built class, to produce fine lines and faster vessels.

The China tea trade gave a great spurt in the early fifties, and from a new source, the Clyde, John Elder & Co. turned out some of the fastest tea clippers that ever had been designed and built.

The race from China to bring the first of the new crop became a sort of oceanic Derby. Some fifty vessels might be ready to start as soon as the first crop was ready for shipment; the moment the early deliveries arrived they were put on board the fastest clippers. Before the last case of tea was on board the crew were aloft loosing sails, and two or three clippers

were waiting breathless to start for the homebound race of some twenty thousand and odd miles to the commercial centre of London.

The homeward course was down the China Sea to the islands off the most westerly province of Dutch Borneo, through the Gaspar Straits between Banka and Billiton islands, to the westward through the Straits of Sunda, which divide Sumatra from Java, passing what remains of Krakatoa, where the terrible volcanic eruption took place in 1883. Then open water to the Cape, and the Cape pigeons will soon welcome them. There the racing clippers may sight each other if very closely matched, if not, possibly in the chops of the English Channel ; for after their 20,000 miles the rival ships have arrived within forty-eight hours of each other. Tradition says the captain of the winner received £500 reward for his achievement, and well deserved it, after constant strain of cracking on through all weathers, sleepless nights, and ceaseless anxiety.

About 1857 the curtain drops on the China clippers. The Suez Canal was opened and the short cut soon left the Cape pigeons undisturbed by their rush.

ENGLAND.

COLLIERS.

ONE of the sights on the River Thames used to be the colliers; those dingy, begrimed brigs which crowded the pool and were closely packed in Bugsby Hole, which lies between Blackwall and Woolwich. All the way down the river, particularly on a flood tide, numbers of the colliers would be met, in strong contrast to the very beautiful and bright-looking Gravesend steamers, with their light green and white looking sides and paddle boxes, which belonged to two rival companies, the Diamond and the Star, watching a competition; for in those days many people went down the river, and amongst them might often have been seen J. W. Turner, returning from Gravesend, with his eyes fixed on the lurid effects of sunset behind the London smoke. As the population of London increased so did the demand for coal; but railways came to the rescue, and eventually steam cleared out the colliers, which had gradually increased in number through the forties. About 1856 steam was replacing the slow and sure old method of conveyance; and our old friends the dingey brigs are unknown to the present generation, if they were not so to the last.

In those days the steamboat travellers on the river must have inhaled a good deal of fine coal-dust as they passed down through an avenue of colliers which were "whipping coals," a process of unloading which is shown in the illustration. A stage was erected over the side of the hold on deck. About five hands were employed, who ran up to lower the scoop into the hold to be filled, and then jumped down to bring up with a run, and shoot the contents into the barge alongside. The East Coast trade was an important nursery for seamen, although there was not much discipline on board these craft; the crew were all sailors brought up and inured to sea life under circumstances of hardship.

The calling of "coal whippers" was so important in the city of London that a "Coal Whippers' Board" was organised to protect the men employed in unloading coals from the rapacity of the longshore publicans, and an Act of Parliament was passed in 1843 for that purpose. There are frequent

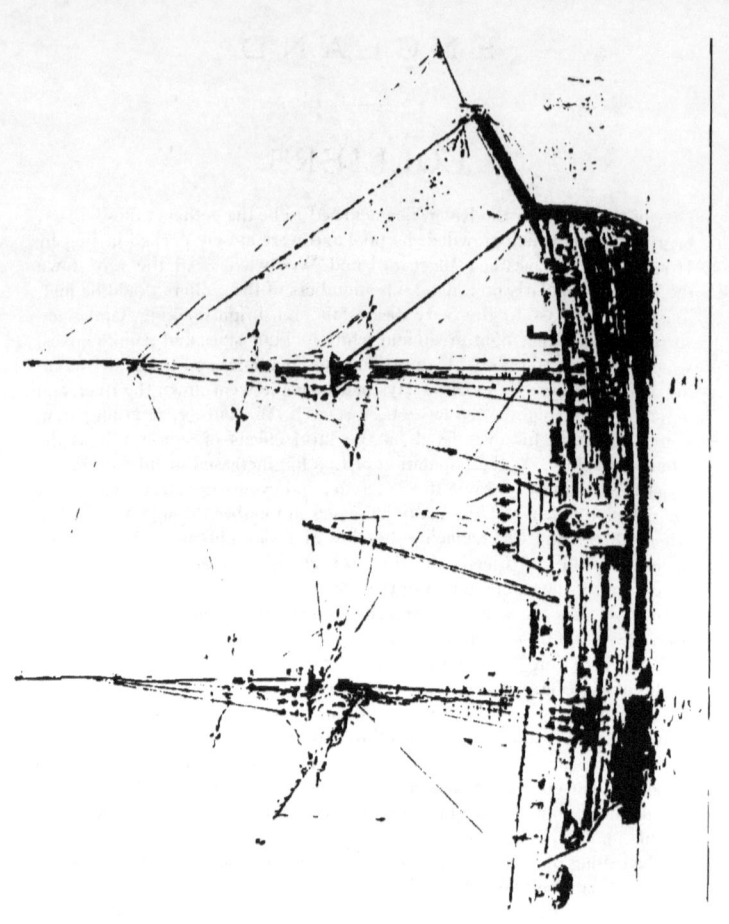

occasions in daily life where "dryness" in the throat is complained of by the operator; in this case there was the terrible combination of an atmosphere of coal-dust, combined with the violent exercise of a rapid treadmill, which rather tempted the Whippers into the clutches of the publicans. In 1856, however, the coalowners themselves established a "whipping" office for the men—it does not sound kind or complimentary until duly understood—and soon afterwards "coal whipping" died a natural death when the railways monopolised the carriage of coals to London. A dying effort was made at Newcastle in 1844, when the old collier brig "Atalanta" was cut in half and steam engines were put into her. The doom of the collier brigs was sealed: half measures were of no use to compete with steam, and in 1852 the "John Bower" was the first steam collier built of iron. This vessel went on running regularly until 1898, when she was broken up.

ENGLAND.

THE YORKSHIRE COBLE.

THE coble is the light boat, typical of the east coast of England from Yarmouth right up north. The build of these boats is very peculiar, combining the two qualities of being well adapted for beaching and yet possessing great power in working to windward. When seen broadside at sea, her sail mast has a severe rake to an angle of about 70°, her gunwale springing towards the stern with a strong rise at the bow before coming to stem. The boats are generally painted with broad bands of colour, light blue, white, and green; the tall mast carrying a narrow lug, with an occasional jib on a temporary bowsprit. The most curious feature is the broad square stern, falling in above and terminating in a flat floor with two keels, locally known as "skirvels," which run up about one third of the length from the stern, making them easy to beach. Forward the entrance is very fine, so to beach her she is put on stern first.

Examining forward, the keel is not one consecutive straight as it comes to the forefoot. Instead of being cut away like modern racing yachts, the keel deepens, giving a great grip for windward, because the rudder goes four feet below the keel, without which the extra depth of forefoot would be a detriment. What anomalies there appear to be in the construction of boats, what play is given to fancy in some of the abortions produced! Here are the dimensions of the classes in general use. The two larger classes, capable of carrying three tons and nine tons, are proportioned:

Length .... 28 ft.   Length .... 33·75.
Beam .... 5 ft. 5 in. Beam .... 10 ft.
Depth .... 2 ft. 3 in. Depth .... 4·75 ft.

These same lines are applied in the small boats carried by the North Sea fishing smacks for cod, ling, and haddock. Each fishing boat, with a crew of five men, carries two small 23-ft. footers, which are clinker built; the others are carvel.

YORKSHIRE COBLES.

Having endeavoured to describe these grand craft- in which the fishermen prefer to go off, rather than in a lifeboat, so thoroughly do they know them and how to handle them—we must leave the thoroughbreds and refer to a recent innovation. At Filey or Scarborough these boats are now built without the double keels or "skirvels," giving them whaler sterns, and the appropriate name of "mules." We think, with the old fishermen, that the "coble" pure is the better craft at sea, the long deep rudder having immense leverage.

"Eheu Fugaces." The last two old cobles at Berwick-on-Tweed suffered so severely in the recent gales that they have since gone to pieces, but there are still some at North Sunderland and Beadnell.

It was in one of the square-sterned cobles that Grace Darling went off to the wreck of the "Forfarshire" steamer from the Outer Farn Island Lighthouse, with her father, the old lighthouse keeper—a feat of daring and dash to save life, about sixty years ago, in 1838, but not yet forgotten; for the coble is still preserved, and was exhibited at the Fisheries Exhibition at South Kensington, in 1886.

ENGLAND.

SAILING BARGES.

THERE is probably no class of vessel so familiar to the eye of the Londoner as a good old-fashioned Medway barge. Colliers have passed away, but the barge holds her own and is still running. It is worth while to go down the river and see the fleet come out of the Medway to catch the young flood to go up the river. The variety of colour in the tanned sails, varying from yellow ochre to deep vandyke brown and madder, offers a grand scheme of colour either to a connoisseur in art or a casual observer. Frequently a new untanned cloth may have been put in, or at other times there may be gaff topsail much the worse for wear and ready for the paper mill—still all picturesque. The pride the skipper takes in his vessel is generally indicated by the art decoration, for barges are gaily painted. The centre of the big sprit which supports the mainsail has generally bands of bright colour, then forward the wash-board has a pattern to match the pattern aft. Their chief characteristic is the lee board, without which she would not be a Medway barge. When we take together the lee board, the bright painting, and the shallowness of draught, we can but come to the conclusion that there is close affinity to the Dutch, with whom large sprit sails were in great favour, and still are. Considering the tonnage and size of a barge, the land lubber can hardly understand the facility with which these craft are navigated, and with how few hands some say a man and a boy, some a man and a dog.

The regular rig is a huge mainsail set with a sprit, so that the canvas is brailed up in a twinkling, a gaff topsail, a mizen with occasionally a mizen staysail set on the long tiller, a foresail and jib this is the true barge. Some years ago barge sailing matches were started, and to see what these craft can do in a hard wind is not only instructive but astonishing. The barges have surprising sea capabilities; they may be seen thrashing through the Downs, battened down, with the deck all amast, smothered in spindrift, just as if they liked it. Latterly some of them come up the river without a bowsprit, setting a jib staysail over the fore-

A MEDWAY BARGE.

sail, but it is an innovation consequent on the ever-increasing traffic on the Thames.

The average tonnage of sailing barges is about 40 register tons, carrying capacity 110 tons ; length, 78 ft. ; beam, 17 ft. ; draught, 6 ft. ; drop of lee board below keel, 8 ft. ; the length of lee board being 12 ft. ; sail area, 400 square yards ; all tanned sails except jib staysail, which is duck.

There is another kind of sailing barge of inferior grade altogether, undecorated and very grimy ; she has no topmast and is therefore called a "dumpy barge."

Commercially the sailing Medway barge holds her own against the railways from Rochester, so that there is much life in them yet. One very picturesque phase is when they appear as hay barges ; they are then a lovely colour, but not quite so lively as when battened down and beating up in the Lower Hope with a heavy cargo.

ENGLAND.

FISHING BOATS.

BRIXHAM TRAWLERS AND PENZANCE LUGGERS.

WESTWARD Ho! brings us to a very fine class of fishing vessels at Torbay. Who has not heard of Brixham trawlers and Berryhead? Brixham is a typical fishing centre, in a lovely situation, looking across Torbay towards Torquay, which, like many other places, is frequently described as the Madeira of England.

When the fleet, numbering some 200 vessels, goes out in the "dumpsey" of the day ("dumpsey" being a Devonshire term for twilight) the crowd of dark-coloured tanned sails produces a very grand effect, the intense depth of tone in the hulls being relieved by the flicker of the fisherman's sidelights, whilst the rich colour of the last crimson of the setting sun catches the upper cirri, the wavelets in the foreground sharing its glory, and throwing the dark mass of the fleet into deeper shade than ever.

The trawlers, when the trawl is hauled, generally get a considerable variety of the finny tribe, large and small; for Brixham supplies such fish as cod, ling, dabs, maguams (a transparent sole with a large head), latchets are large gurnards, without the dorsal fin, running up to 9lb.; red mullet, the woodcock of the sea; skate, rock salmon or bass, plaice, which so frequently become filleted soles on the breakfast table at hotels; red gurnards with spikey whiskers and dorsal fins; hake, a fish not much thought of many years ago but now reviving in public estimation; rock whiting, sea bream, Torbay soles, lemon soles, the noble turbot, the pleasant brill, the fierce conger. Conger and hake are the only fish that induce the fisher to take with him a policeman's truncheon with a little lead in the end, to give the victim a quick and speedy end. To finish the list, we conclude with the most curious, grotesque-looking fish that we have on our coasts, the John Dory (*Zeus faber*). These fish sometimes run on shore; they are slothful and lazy. The writer was bathing at Bognor some years ago and saw a John Dory in the water in a slothful frame of mind evidently. Having taken bearings, he landed for a boat-hook, and after a long stalk found "Mr. John," provided him behind the gill, and carried him home on the boat-hook. For the rest of his visit the fishermen were frequently heard to say, "There goes the 'John Dory' gent."

But the above-named fish by no means represent the whole contents of

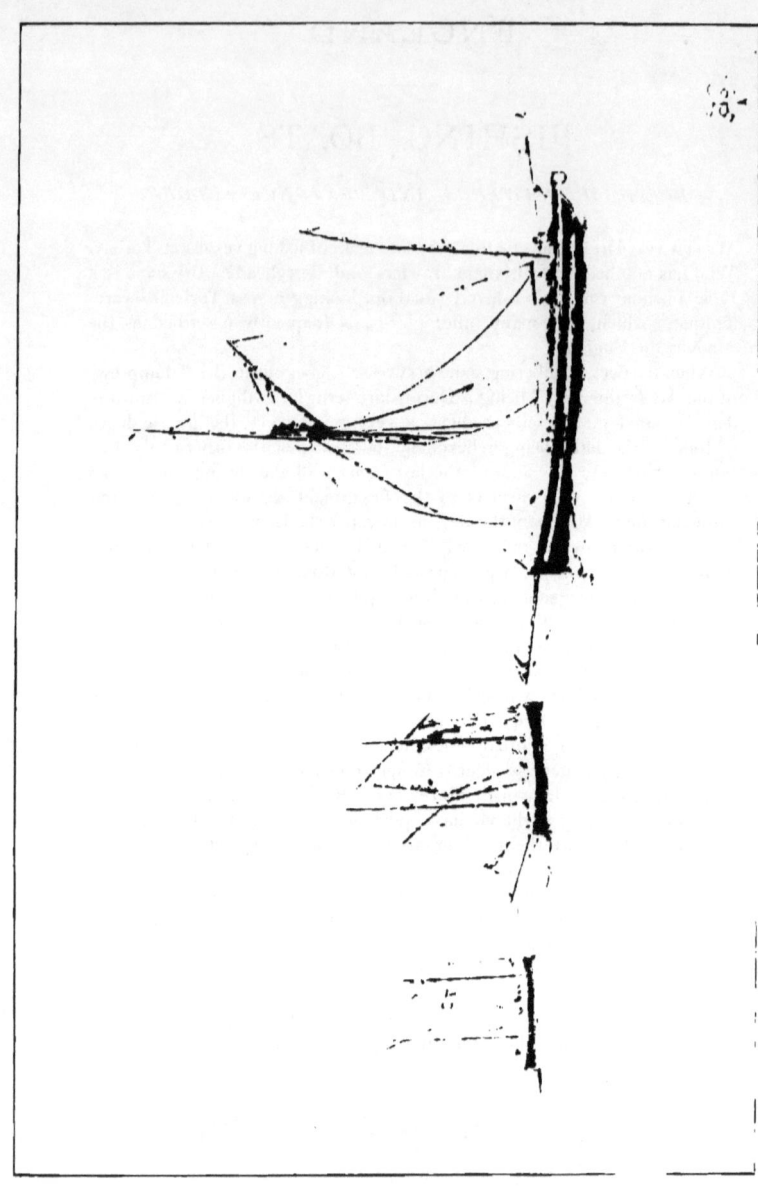

MANX AND PENZANCE FISHING BOATS AND BRIXHAM TRAWLER.

the trawl. Dog fish, sea mice, squids and creeping things innumerable afford great scope for the deep-sea student and microscopic research.
The vessels themselves are very powerful boats of 60 tons; crew of four; S. A. 900 square ft.; length over all, 70 ft.; beam, 18 ft.; draught, 10 ft. aft, forward 9 ft.; length of trawl beam, 45 ft.

Their tan-coloured sails are always picturesque, and they never look better than when, with the trawl down, they are regulating their speed with a huge reaching stay-sail sheeted right aft. Brixham is certainly one of the chief fishing towns of England.

Going further west beyond Plymouth, the Penzance luggers attract attention from their beautiful lines and the great jigger which comes out over the stern like a huge sting. We are now in the pilchard district, and what a delicious fish it is, much richer than his close relation, the herring. Although such thousands are taken, how few reach the metropolis, and how seldom is it seen on a menu card! A good pilchard season is a real boon to the men of Cornwall. The pilchard itself is considered to be a full-grown sardine; and, oddly enough, great quantities of these are prepared *à la sardine* in oil, and sent to the Mediterranean: for home use they are simply salted. Directly the fish are expected great preparations are made. The great seine is carefully examined; the huer, or lookout man, gets his instructions where to go on the cliff to signal their arrival and direction. The seine boat, with a second boat called the "Volyer," carry two lugs, whilst a third boat, known as the "Lurker," is a handy little spritsail boat which acts as galloper to the commander-in-chief. The "master seiner" is a very high post indeed. At Penzance these fish are called "fair maids," and when one hears a visitor order a couple of "fair maids" for breakfast, one's thoughts turn towards Fiji or the Solomon Islands. Before leaving Penzance and turning our backs on the lovely object, St. Michael's Mount, we must give the dimensions of the Penzance luggers, about 27 tons, the jigger always to port; length, 47 ft.; beam, 13·5 ft.; draught, 7 ft. To see them racing is a splendid sight; such spinnakers and contrivances to sail their pets a bit harder.

In one of these yawl-rigged boats E. F. Knight started with a Corinthian crew to go round the world in 1879.

The Isle of Man affords very good fishing off a "Bahama Bank," some six or seven miles off Ramsey, not sufficient, however, to keep the Manx fishermen in their own waters. Their boats run rather larger than the Penzance craft. Some of the finest are most powerful boats, hailing from Castletown, with "C. T." on the bow; they are as much as 54 tons, with a length of 56 ft. and 14·75 ft. beam. The difference of their rig is that they are very fond of a staysail, the stay leading from halfway up the main topmast to the foot of the foremast, otherwise they might be taken for Mount Bay or Penzance boats, as their jiggers are in the same proportion.

ENGLAND.

LIGHTSHIPS AND LIFEBOATS.

To understand the value of lighthouses and lightships a glance should be taken at a wreck chart—for a glance is quite enough—to see the number of wrecks which annually occur all round our coasts. Then we should appreciate the benefit which the Trinity House has conferred on our shipping interests, and the importance of that valuable institution, whilst our thoughts must recur to the days when wreckers burnt false lights to bring to destruction the unwary. The Trinity House was originally an association for piloting ships, as early as 1512, and Henry VIII. did much to encourage pilots at Newcastle, Hull, and Deptford, by establishing fraternities or guilds for them. In the present time a "Trinity pilot" retains all the dignity of earlier days. He has passed his examination, secured his licence, and thoroughly deserves his official position.

The earliest lights were probably cressets, the kind of light used on shore to guide wayfarers; one of these used to be in the church at Barnet. Tynemouth Castle in Northumberland was well known as a lighthouse in the time of Charles I. The great light on the Eddystone rock off Plymouth was the first important and real lighthouse, especially associated with the name of Smeaton, who built it of stone about 1759. There are the two celebrated lighthouses, the North and South Foreland, and the "Lizard," especially important as the point from which ships take their departure and lay their course; it is a magnificent light of great range, and looms for miles beyond its true light-radius. For the last twenty years the magneto-electric light has been used with great success, after experiments had been tried with earlier forms of it at Dungeness and the South Foreland lighthouses.

The Trinity House on Tower Hill has some interesting models of early lights and lighthouses and ships; and especially of the first Nore lightship, only 80 ft. long and about one hundred tons, of the date 1732. She was moored with huge hemp cables, and the lights consisted of two

THE "CORK" LIGHTSHIP AND TURBINE LIFEBOAT OFF HARWICH.

candles, one in each lanthorne at the end of the yard ; to lower, then relight and hoist, requires a cunning arrangement, with an alteration in the position of the shrouds. The starboard shrouds are before the mast and the port ones abaft the mast, so that the yard can be hoisted quite square to the mast and at right angles to the keel.

The rig of lightships varies, some of them having three, two, or one mast, according to the number of lights displayed. The single masted are most general. They are always painted red and coppered ; the light which is round the mast is hoisted by very strong tackles, and every part of the vessel is constructed for strength to resist the most severe storms possible. They are generally moored with mushroom anchors ; it is very seldom that a case occurs where they drag. Some two or three years ago the " Warner " lightship dragged in a southerly gale, but fortunately it was only a short distance to the Hampshire coast. All lightships are rigged with a mizen, for the purpose of keeping their head to the wind, and instead of the old gong and foghorn, a syren is now generally shipped, whilst at stations like the Start Point, Lizard, and South Foreland, steam syrens are separate establishments close to the light.

The steam lifeboat came out about 1889, with the great advantage of being on the " turbine " principle, and of not having any propeller which might get entangled with the rigging of floating topmasts or other cordage. The turbine system was very successful also as to speed, getting nine knots out of a boat when in sea-going trim on active service, with full complement of crew on board and a sufficient coal supply. For canvas she carries a trysail and staysail, also oars as a third motor if the others fail. The boat represented was the " Duke of Northumberland," being named after the president of The National Lifeboat Institution. She looks unmistakably a lifeboat all round, with her life lines all round her and the usually distinctive colouring. Her length was about 50 ft., built by Messrs. Green of Blackwall, who describe her as a " hydraulic steam lifeboat."

The National Lifeboat Institution was founded in 1824, but as early as 1790 there was a great stir made at South Shields to get a successful model to adopt. Mr. Lukin had tried an iron keel to ballast them, and one was launched at Bamborough Head and saved lives. South Shields, however, was the first place to found lifeboats as a national requirement, and the lifeboats of our present Institution saved as many as 1,048 lives from shipwreck in the year of grace 1877.

ICEBOATS.

THE iceboats of Holland must be accepted as the *doyennes* of the family. Holland is so generally acknowledged as an ice school, with its variety of gorgeous sledges, fast skaters, "kermesses" on the ice. Even fishing is added to the ice sports, when the enthusiastic piscator, having made a hole in the ice, puts up a weather screen and settles down with plenty of aniseed and milk, possibly a little Schnapps pocket pistol in case of more severe weather coming on, and makes up his mind to simple enjoyment of a piscatorial existence.

Our English climate, thanks to the genial influence of the Gulf Stream, does not favour the pastime of iceboat sailing, much less does it encourage it. Windermere is a spot where the sport is in full force directly Jack Frost gives a chance.

Iceboats are undoubtedly a specialty in North America. An Iceboat Club was formed and known as the "Poughkeepsie" Ice Yacht Club of America. Yacht club is a term which hardly coincides with our idea of the term yacht, as that implies a pleasure vessel in which the owner can live and sleep, whereas the craft in which the owner cannot live and sleep have been most appropriately named in America "day boats." The modern iceboat is to all intents and purposes really a day boat.

The day of small boats has passed away, and as speed develops with sail area and sail area necessitates length, so the iceboats have increased in length of body to 68 ft., with 1,000 square feet of canvas. This seems a small amount of canvas when we think that the Sydney boat in Australia is only 24 feet in length, with 1,000 square feet of canvas in fine weather. The pace attained, however, is very different, consequent on the difference of resistance between water and the icy surface. From all accounts, the pace of the ice yachts racing under favourable circumstances and close hauled must be terrific, and practical comparisons are made by racing with the trains as they run down the side of the Hudson River. The body of the ice yacht is really a framework in the form of a cross, travelling on three steel runners, one at each end of the cross piece to give stability, the third right aft as a rudder. The mast is placed in front of the cross piece

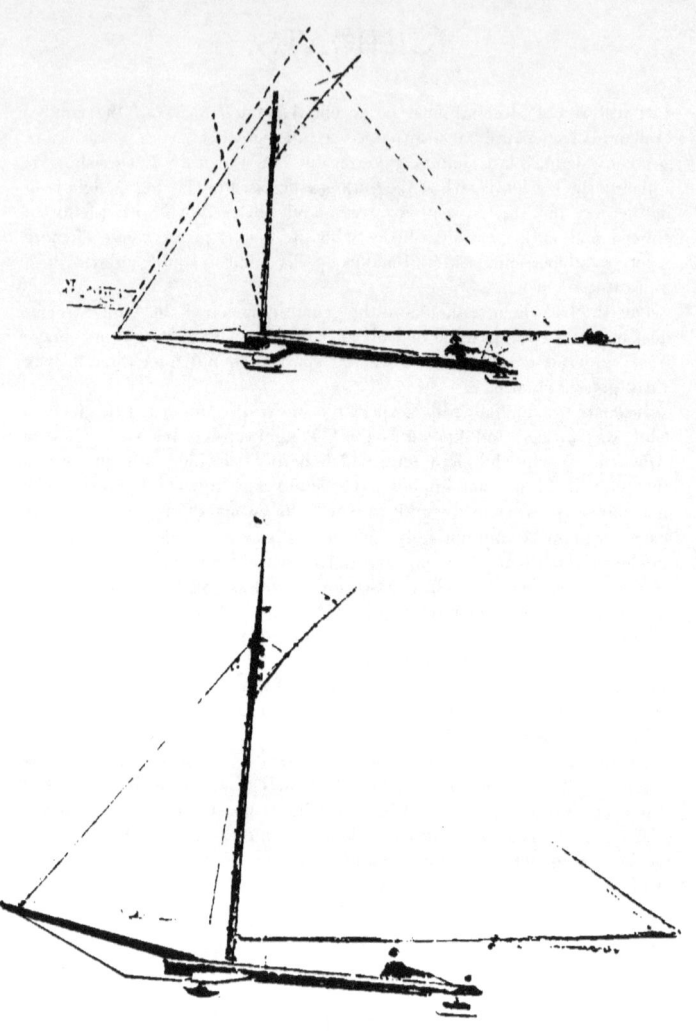

ICE BOATS ON THE HUDSON AND AT ST. MORITZ.

and securely fixed by stays to the outer ends, port and starboard, of the runner plank.

Up to twenty years ago the Shrewsbury River boats had four runners and were very fast going, free, and very safe. The Hudsons have the honour of introducing pace to windward. Commodore Grinnell has published a work, "Laws of Ice Navigation," from which the iceboat enthusiast may learn much, especially on beating to windward, when the greatest speed is attained. The following are the measurements of an iceboat, first class, on Hudson River :—

Centre timber over all, 52 ft. ; rudder post to centre of runner plank, 27 ft. ; beam, 28 ft. ; sail area, 911 sq. ft. Sloop rig and under all circumstances "sheets flat aft." Season, December 1st to March 31st.

The exciting moment in these races is when the weather runner lifts, then the balance is critical and more live ballast is wanted on that runner.

At St. Moritz the American Club boats are carefully imitated and very successfully, so that the description of the American sport applies in a smaller degree to the limited sport of St. Moritz, where there is no Hudson River, no Shrewsbury River, to race over against "lightning express trains."

THE UNITED STATES.

YACHTS.

THE " VIGILANT " AND " VALKYRIE."

AMERICAN centre-board boats have been for many years quite a national feature. Started originally in consequence of the shallow coasts, where keel boats would be handicapped, they were the outcome of the early form of those primitive boxes or boats which the fowler used to sink as a screen when after wild fowl along the sandbanks on the coast of New York Bay and the New Jersey coasts. Adapting themselves to surrounding circumstances, which Americans so readily do, the boxes were lengthened, finally becoming what were called "scows," or floating blinds, very much like the wild fowl "blinds" used by the Dutch in the winter time on the sea. When the corners were rounded off, these "scows" became boats; and to give stability in deeper water a hand-board was dropped down through a well slot; the board was not hinged in any way, and soon acquired the name of "dagger boards." Such was the beginning, a hundred years ago, of centre-boards, and now, in looking over the catalogue of models in the New York Yacht Club, which numbers 289 specimens, 159 are centre-board yachts. The numerous steam yachts included in the catalogue do not require them, and the crack racers for the America Cup have now settled down to keel boats, the races being run in deep water. The "Vigilant" and "Valkyrie" contest was one of the most exciting races on record. Sailed in a hard wind, with every stitch of canvas they could set, the marvel is that nothing was carried away, although a big sloop was dismasted just at the time which the sketch represents. When we know that "Vigilant" had a sail area of 12,330 square feet on a water line of 86.19 ft. our wonder must increase.

Lord Dunraven's "Valkyrie" was unfortunate at the start of the first race; the wind was so light that their spinnakers hardly drew, and at the first mark "Valkyrie" led, and at five o'clock the committee sent up the recall flag, so that was no race. October is not a good month for a race of such interest, the wind being very light and flukey. A true wind of good strength is wanted for the windward work.

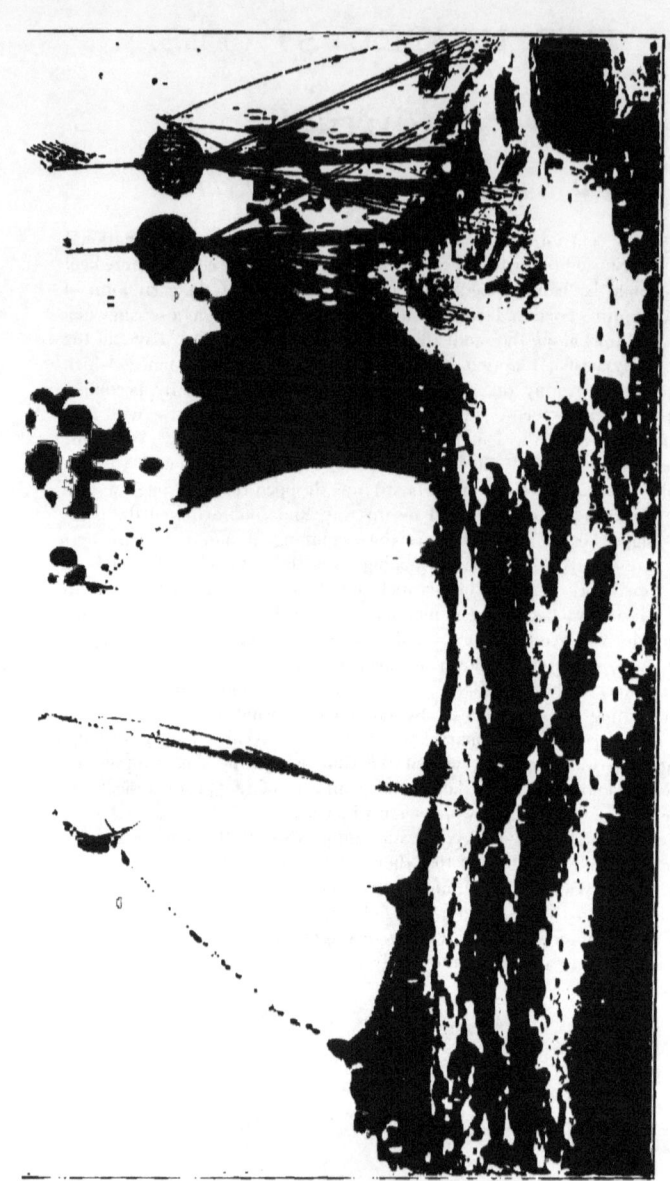

THE AMERICA CUP.

The "Vigilant" winning from the "Valkyrie."

On the fifth day, October 13, 1893, there was a great change; the weather became overcast and the wind S.E., blowing moderately when they started from Sandy Hook. "Valkyrie" passed the line at 12 hours 27 minutes, off Long Island she was on "Vigilant's" weather, going well and standing well up to her canvas, both yachts starting with jib-headers, "Valkyrie" leading at the mark, after rounding, "down spinnaker booms" for the run home. "Valkyrie" setting her very biggest balloon jib topsail, to which "Vigilant" responded with that excellent and favourite sail in America, a balloon bowsprit spinnaker. The run home was most exciting, and on board the "Vigilant" some fine canvas handling was shown : for instance, they began by shaking out the reef in the mainsail, which was splendidly done. Finding she would stand being sailed a little harder, they sent up their jack-yarder over the jib-headed gaff-topsail as shewn in the sketch—in America they generally have double topsail halyards. This extra canvas enabled them to run through "Valkyrie's" lee and to win a race splendidly sailed by both yachts.

We mentioned that "Valkyrie" was unfortunate : when the "Vigilant's" jack-yarder went up the "Valkyrie's" spinnaker burst. It was very smartly handled, and another set, but only to share the same fate, and to be replaced by a large jib topsail, which was not enough. In another eight minutes the race was over, the wind increasing at the finish.

	hrs.	mins.	secs.	
"Vigilant" finishing... ...	3	51	39	centre-board.
"Valkyrie" ,, ...	... 3	53	52	keel.

"Vigilant" gaining before the wind and "Valkyrie" on the wind—the latter considered the higher quality of the two.

Commodore Stevens with his little 51-footer schooner "Gimcrack," was the founder of the New York Yacht Club in July, 1844, and on a motion "it was resolved that the club do make a cruise to Newport, Rhode Island, under the command of the Commodore."

The American general rig has been schooners for yachts—and fine craft they were ; but the evolution of yachting has displaced them for the facility of locomotion afforded by steam. The same has occurred in this country, where the noble schooners like "Narifa" and "Kestrel" have been replaced by steam yachts of larger tonnage, some of the later of them, such as "Eros" and "Giralda," being almost like mail-steamers-de-luxe, whilst the steam yachts on the other side run to much larger tonnage, Mr. Howard Gould's steam yacht "Niagara" being 1,900 tons, and Mr. Vanderbilt's steam yacht "Valiant" 2,300 tons.

Although the English cutters have been taken up in America for racing, still the schooner rig for large yachts, and cat boats for small ones have been their natural features.

THE UNITED STATES.

COASTING SCHOONERS.

BEFORE describing the very interesting and curious river barge, we must say a few words about the American Mercantile Marine, which was so ably represented by a large class, generally known as Baltimore clippers, with flaring bows and any amount of extra sticks and twigs in the form of "sliding gunters." They had a great day until the evil time when they had to succumb to steam.

Down south for coasting purposes schooners were used of all dimensions. The general idea of a schooner is that of a vessel with two masts, carrying square sails on the fore, and a gaff topsail and mainsail on the main. In America, fore and afters are the usually adopted rig : owners do not, however, confine themselves to two-masted schooners, or even as we do. They tried and adopted four-masters, and some five-masters, the "Governor Ames" for instance. The reason for this is the great saving in the number of hands required to work the vessel, because all sheets work on horses across the deck ; and when the schooner goes about, over they go, without any helping hand from the crew. A very bold, fine four-masted schooner was built in 1896 at Port Glasgow, to go out to Honolulu in the Sandwich Islands, intended for the timber trade. In a vessel of this kind the economy of labour is surprising with the sheets of the fore and aft canvas. Two or three men tend the sheets ; these, with a man at the wheel, suffice to carry out all the duties of a watch, whilst the heavy work, such as at the start, getting the anchor, and setting the canvas, is done by the auxiliary power of a steam winch.

Some of the small schooners down to Bahamas and Nassau are very pretty craft indeed, and when the fleet of sponge schooners start off to their happy hunting grounds at Eleuthera it is a delightful sight. At Nassau, the English Bishop went round his diocese in a hundred-ton schooner, which looked a most inviting conveyance. He described to me some of his flock at Bemini, who were considered wreckers, as quite delightful to go amongst.

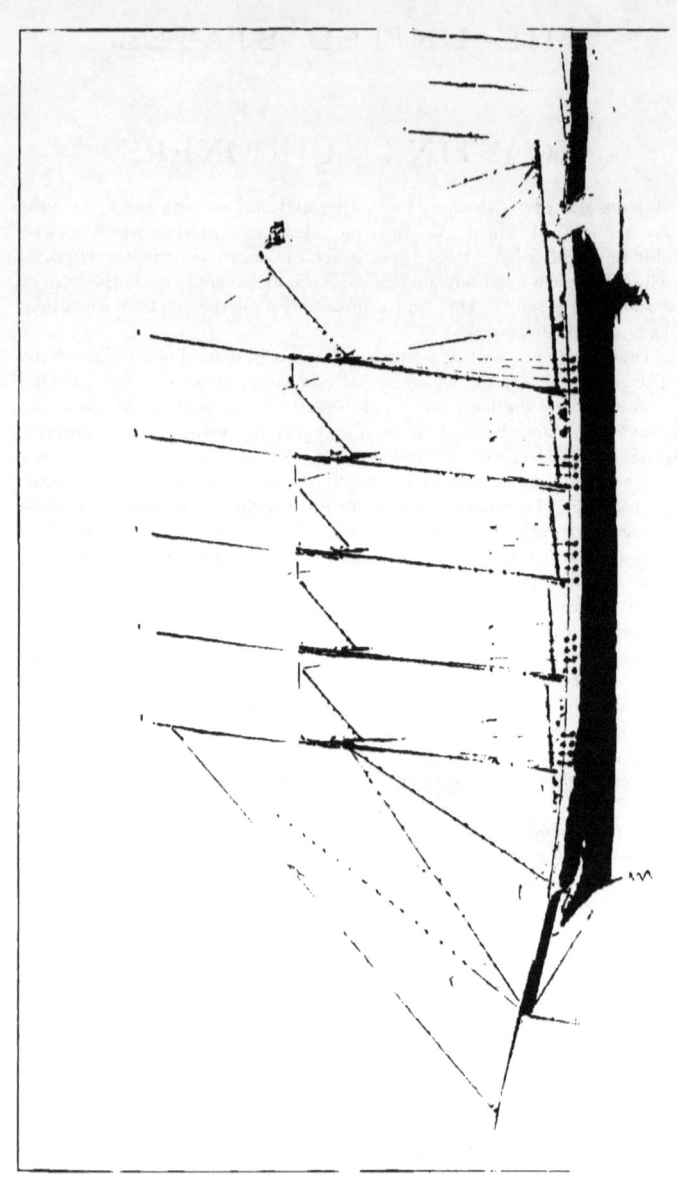

They would do anything for him ; others they would do for in the twinkling of an eye.

Vessels of this kind are a novelty in this country, not so along the West Coast of America, where they are to be seen running up to 2,000 tons. The "Honolulu," built at Port Glasgow on the Clyde, was constructed of steel, and during the process of building was an object of much interest, as so large a schooner had never been previously built in this country. She was built to the order of her owner in Honolulu by Messrs. Duncan and Co., who imparted to her many American features of the schooner class of her sisters away West, and at the same time the characteristics of the old Yankee clippers, which were notorious for their fine sheer sharp bows, with a flare above the fine water lines, tall masts, and a plentiful spread of canvas. The Yankee clippers were in their prime in the forties, and our China tea clippers flourished in the fifties of this century. Not only is the hull steel, but the masts also are of the same material, standing all at the same length, 140 ft. to the truck, with a diameter of 27 ins. at the deck. The hull has been constructed in the very strongest way possible, to carry the immense weight of timber, of which her cargo will consist when on coast work. It is difficult to realise a schooner, a fore-and-after, 225 ft. over all, with a beam of 42 ft., depth of hold 18 ft. 6 in., which naturally gives her high bulwarks. The two large ports in the stern are to receive the timber, as seen in the Norwegian timber ships which come over to this country, and generally have a windmill going to pump out the water. The "Honolulu" has not this appliance, being watertight, which the Norwegian timber ships never are ; in fact, when their skippers come on shore it is considered a compliment to place a shallow tub of water under the dining table to make them feel quite cared for and welcome, as they sit with their feet in it.

THE UNITED STATES.

RIVER BARGES.

THE GUNDALOW.

THIS old looking barge is nearly "the last of the Mohicans." Where could its design have originated? It is certainly a lateen sail, and, if the end of the yard were hauled in close to the mast, it would be a Bermudian. There is no doubt but that it is a *bonâ fide* sail set on a yard, which, being heavily weighted at the lower end and balanced, can be lowered on deck. This yard reminds one at once of the balanced well-poles in Holland and Belgium and Egypt ; also of the well balanced masts in Dutch schuyhts, which bow their heads so snugly to the bridges of Holland. For river work it has done well in its day ; it has now become a curiosity, as only two or three of them remain on active service.

So too the little " Pinkey," the local name of small off-shore fishing schooners from Maine. She too is almost extinct. Her high stern is very characteristic ; in fact the bow of the barge seems quite foreign to the United States. Can it have any association with her local name, which oddly enough is a " Gundalow"? The reef points too are in a very unusual position for a lateen sail, so that the whole arrangement seems to be a cosmopolitan conglomeration.

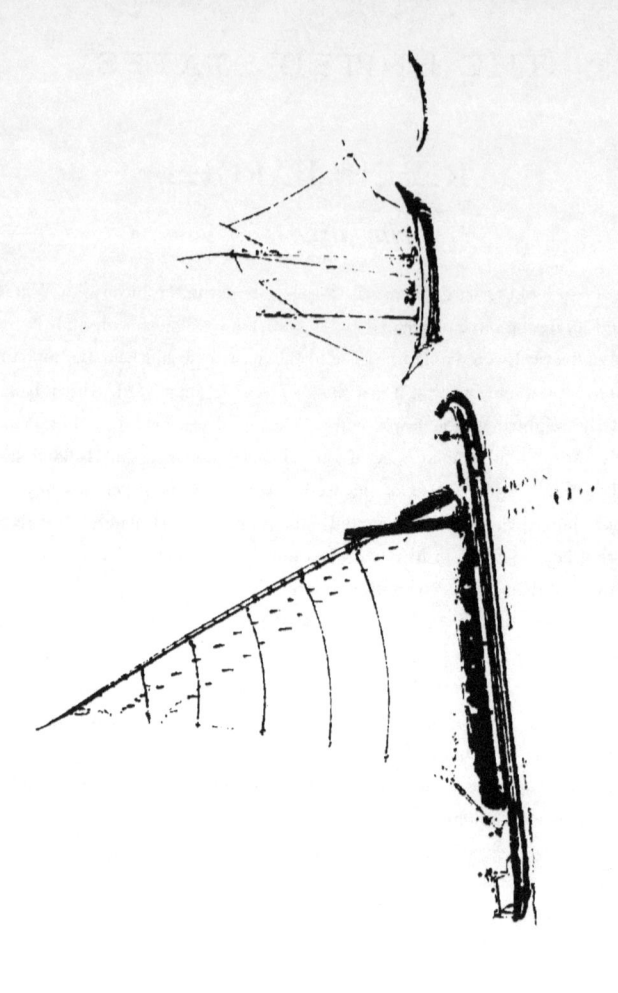

The little boat in tow from the stern of the "Pinkey" is called a "Dorey," a generic name of almost all boats used to go over to an island. "Let us go in the Dorey." How large these Doreys are dependent saith not, but my friend in Rhode Island, Lewis Herreshoff, gave me these technicals, which are very interesting to record at this time, when old things so rapidly pass away and new things crowd upon us, in spite of the fact that there is nothing new under the sun, except in combination.

BERMUDA.

THE BERMUDA RIG.

BERMUDA sailing boats have been long famous in their own *habitat*. They do not seem to transplant to advantage—it may be for want of proper handling—as yet they are not a success in our home waters. They have been tried on the Clyde, at Plymouth, and in the Solent without success.

The Bermudian rig is very noticeable; first the extreme height of the pole mast, to the head of which the mainsail tapers up; next the long boom passes before and past the mast with a tackle to haul it back to flatten the sail, whilst the main sheet keeps it down till all is taut—in fact, the mainsail gives the idea of a mainsail and jack-yarder all in one. The true Bermuda type is generally about five tons: length, 25 ft.; beam, about 7 ft.; the mast, 44 ft.; the boom, 33 ft.; bowsprit, 19 ft. The hull is constructed of cedar; in Bermuda all is cedar and onions. Many are the cedar coffins exported, and if a Bermudian wishes to pay you a great compliment you are called an "onion." Perhaps it was an ephemeral term and has since passed away; still, the complimentary epithet had its day, and a long one too.

These boats mostly have a plate on the keel, not a centre-board, and are fast on a wind. Fortunately the weather is generally very moderate, so much so that there is no chance of reefing her down, for the sail is generally lashed to the mast-head, not hoisted. In case of an untimely puff, the only chance is to "luff her up" smartly before the squall catches, or over she must go.

When running they set a square-headed spinnaker, which is of enormous size, almost rivalling the spread of muslin shown in the Royal Sydney yachts of 24 ft. in length. The best fun, however, for true " water babies " is racing in the dinghey class, little open boats of 14 ft. in length, open of course, probably with a mast twice her own length. The canvas can be imagined, to balance which live ballast is shipped, consisting of five enthusiasts, who are prepared to swim for their lives without any notice. Once on board, all are carefully packed to balance the nutshell, and then they are pushed off. Manœuvring for the start creates great excitement amongst the spectators, and if no more than one turns turtle it is voted rather tame. For all that, it is rare fun, and the performers are generally very accomplished in the art of dinghey-sailing with live ballast.

AUSTRALIA.

SYDNEY.

SYDNEY FLYING SQUADRON.

WHAT a change now from those early days when Botany Bay represented all the British public knew of this vast continent, a bay christened with a name so simple and peaceful that it seemed unnatural to associate it with penal servitude and punishment for crime. Discovered by Cook, he gave it the name of Botany Bay from the number and variety of flowers which were found growing on the shore. That was on April 28, 1770. Some eighteen years afterwards our Government transplanted thither 800 convicts, about 200 of whom were women, and settled them down in a lovely climate at Port Jackson, deeming it a good site for future development; and, indeed, most successful and remarkable has been its rapid growth and prosperity. The descendants of the first settlers are now only known as Government people, and the wild oats of their ancestors forgotten. Port Jackson is now Sydney, the capital of New South Wales, so named after Lord Sydney, a Secretary for the Colonies.

Sydney is now the heart of Australia, and the only aborigines to be met with are the Port Jackson sharks, with their complicated dental construction; and even they are becoming less vicious than they used to be.

In Sydney and the lovely bay yachting has taken firm root. In the Colonies there must be a struggle before it can even get a footing, for yachting is always an outcome of prosperity, being a rather expensive amusement, and Colonial life puts business before pleasure.

Sydney is the Cowes of Australia, and has two prominent yacht clubs, founded thirty years ago—the Royal Sydney Yacht Squadron in 1863, and the Prince Alfred Yacht Club in 1867. Boat sailing has naturally been carried on to a great extent for many years. What Englishman could resist the temptation of such a splendid cruising ground of about twelve

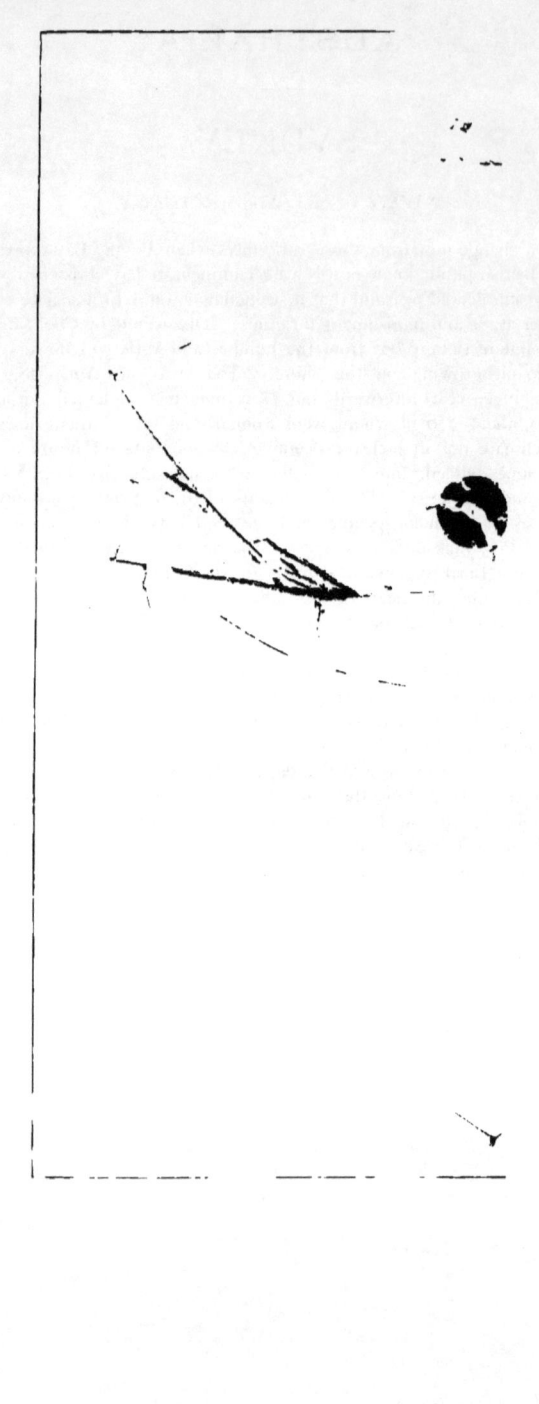

square miles lying inside the Port Jackson Heads? The enthusiasts have backed their hobby well, with great thoroughness. Not content with local talent, they sought the assistance of the best designers, G. L. Watson and Fife, of English fame, and even Nat. G. Herreshoff has not been forgotten. The great water sport of Sydney is, however, sailing the open boats with live ballast, plenty of canvas, plenty of ballast, and "never mind the sharks." *Experientia docet.* With one class of boat, and continual practice under similar conditions, it is surprising to see how the boats are handled, how nippily the live ballast finds its place when gybing, how rapidly the canvas is taken in or set—a very important function, for the winds in the bay are treacherous and uncertain, the most favourable being hard north-easters. Crossing the mouth of the harbour sometimes gives the adventurers a very nasty shake up, and the baling is rapid, with great earnestness. To get to the water to bale is a feat in itself in a boat 24 ft. long, with 22 men as crew for ballast—44 legs in the bottom of the boat. Here discipline comes in, the crew sit double banked, and all lower extremities are stowed close up to the gunwale on each side.

This description of the favourite boat in Sydney applies to a boat brought over to the mother country in 1898 to challenge for a race against the same length of boat; although the word challenge is scarcely applicable, the owner coming from pure love of sport, carrying out everything connected with the five races sailed in the same fine manly spirit of fairness. The races were sailed in September, 1898, in the Medway, certainly not under favourable conditions. In the first place, the visitors, Mr. M. Fay and crew "Irex," were not accustomed to a tideway; secondly, the English boat, Mr. Wyllie's "Maid of Kent," was a decked boat of shallow type, designed by Linton Hope. There were no gentle zephyrs to woo the full expanse of canvas, 1,000 square ft., with which "Irex" is generally garbed in the home waters of her beautiful Bay of Sydney, consequently the "Maid of Kent" won, but only with one result—that this contest became a new tie of interest between Australia, with Sydney as head quarters, and the mother country.

NORWAY.

JAEGTS AND FISHING CRAFT.

THE vast seaboard of Norway naturally produces a class of men inured to the hardships of the coast work of the country, where the whole line is iron-bound ; even the fjords which run inland for a great distance afford poor anchorage. Such is the depth of the water close up to the precipitous coast, that iron rings may still be seen in some parts where the boats were literally tied up to the rocks. Travelling by boat is much easier than conveying weighty loads over the mountains from one village to the other, and Norway has in this case the very great advantage of the warmth of the Gulf Stream running up the whole length of the coast, with the comforting effect that in the winter time no ice is seen at sea, although plenty can be found in view, and on shore mighty glaciers too, as the traveller looks up to Justerdal and other snow ranges.

The Norwegian jaegt, the national type of vessel on the coast, is quite a relic of bygone days, with her one big square sail ; her build with high stern, the same as two hundred years ago : her high black stem, now without the figure or head of former days at the summit ; her lines faithful to those handed down from the Viking period. A perfect specimen of a boat of that period was discovered some years ago, and is now treasured at Christiana. This type of vessel is employed to bring the immense supply of fish from the Lofoden Islands—where the cod fishery of Norway is concentrated—and down the coast to Bergen, whence it is shipped off to the Mediterranean. The vessels that bear away the fish generally return with cargoes of wine, and this direct importation supplies a want, to the agreeable surprise of many a traveller. The tradition was, and may be still, that these vessels came down to Bergen laden with dried fish, and on their return had a cargo of elm planks for coffins, calling on their way up to distribute these *memento mori*.

The jaegt is not unfrequently in request for a Norwegian bridal party, as shown in the illustration. Then are the fiddles and the tankards much in

NORWEGIAN JAEGT AND FISHING BOAT

evidence. The high poop is rigged up as an arbour for the bride to sit in, in gorgeous array in her national costume, with the old silver ornaments and brooches and chains to lace the bodice, the whole surmounted by the bridal crown of silver gilt. Some of these crowns are of great antiquity and very beautiful design, most of them with hinges so that they can be folded. By her side the happy bridegroom generally looks somewhat demure, although a little proud of his surroundings and the honours paid on the occasion. Below, on the main deck, are constant sounds of "Skaal!" "Skaal!" or health, for the tankards have not a minute's peace at these times; often and often are they filled and refilled. The tankards are generally made of wood, carved with inscriptions; the favourite lion is frequently introduced on the handle, and round the rim or base may be words of good advice, such as, "Of me you must drink but swear not, nor ever drink too much," "Drink me forthwith and be thankful, for I shall soon be no more." At these times, the Norwegian songs are heard in praise of "Höje Fjelde" and the beautiful mountain scenery; the words frequently of Björnson, and music by Kjerulf, a favourite composer. When the shore is reached there is much powder expended, and the national spring dance crowns the proceedings at rather a late hour for such simple people. Such are the varied duties of these grand old craft; stoutly built, they last for years and years, and as yet they are not being pushed into oblivion by aggressive steamers.

NORWAY.

NORWEGIAN HERRING BOATS.

The small boats of Norway were, till the last few years, the only means of getting along this very iron-bound coast; and those who really wish to see the grandeur of the coast scenery would do well to remember how delightful it is to start with one of these for an expedition, well provided with fladbrod, smör, and that most important item for the four-oared crew, sundry bottles of Ol, which is the welcome beer. It is surprising how the boatmen will go on and on at their never-tiring, steady travelling stroke, now and then, particularly after rations and Ol, bursting out with some of their delightful Norwegian songs.

There is a good deal of the old sea-rover spirit still left amongst them. In one long boat expedition we were making, suddenly, as we rounded a bluff point, Bow in great excitement jumped up, and exclaimed, "Sea rovers ahead, there," pointing to the horizon, where we could see no foe, then he banged his oar down into the rowlock, to represent "the first shot" into them. Then the others took up the joke, and fought the ship all round, and ere long announced that the sea rover was sunk, and we went on our way rejoicing.

Boat expeditions should not be neglected, for the Norwegians are natural mariners; living on such a rocky, precipitous coast they must master the arts of the sea or submit to be landlocked. A good Norwegian herring boat would be a good cruiser if time were no object. This class of boat varies much in size, although the rig is never altered, much less discarded: one of the smaller ones would be about 35 ft. in length, with a beam of 9 ft., depth 3 ft.: the mast 25 ft. in height, with a yard for the mainsail, probably 12 ft. The mainmast is placed half way between perpendiculars, and the sail has two rows of reef points in the head of the sail, and one row at the foot. Reef lines run down the edge of the sail through cringles in the bolt rope, and the foot of the sail is held down by a crow-foot bridle

NORWEGIAN HERRING BOATS.

to prevent it roaching. The parrels round the mast from the yard are unusual, being alternately long and short, so that the short one revolves as the sail is hoisted or lowered, the long ones acting as guides. The tiller is very long, with a downward spring to press in and remain fixed between a line of pegs placed thwart ship.

The row boats are the same type all up the coast, and similar to the one in Plate, where the two "pigers" are pulling their hardest to reach the bridal party. Ships from Christiana Fjord often carry a small boat called in this country a Norway punt, probably because the nose of the boat is cut off square.

A great many timber ships come over to England, and are generally easily picked out by the small windmill going round abaft the mainmast, performing a duty very frequently imperative in these vessels, though timber laden -that of pumping on a large scale. This trade of larger barge sailing ships is giving way to steamers, which are frequently now seen coming out of the North Sea with a tremendous list, enough to frighten any landsman.

DENMARK.

DANISH COASTER.

THERE is a strong family likeness running all through the coasters of Denmark, mostly of the sloop family; the sloop having one mast, standing bowsprit, and a jibboom for head sails; a long yard carries a flying square sail, whilst the yard for the topsail is generally sent up as occasion may require; a boom mainsail and gaff topsail completes the rig. These sloops are something between the Dutch and the Norwegian jaegt build, with plenty of sheer and beam, consequently good sea boats, and stand up well to their canvas in a hard wind.

In size and appearance they much resemble the billy-boys of our east coast. They, like other local craft, are rapidly giving way to the steam "tramps," a modern name for cargo-carrying steamers.

All over the Baltic these sloops are found, carrying goods to small places which have not yet developed to the steamboat pier stage.

Although the Dogger bank is so near, very few Danish craft are seen there, the distance up round the Skaw or entrance to the Baltic being so far. Most of the "herringers" go to the island of Anholt, where the shoals favour the fishing, and fishing boats assemble there from all parts of the Sound, starting early in August for their season.

Copenhagen has lately taken up yachting rather vehemently, stimulated by the presence of some resident Englishmen. There is a splendid cruising

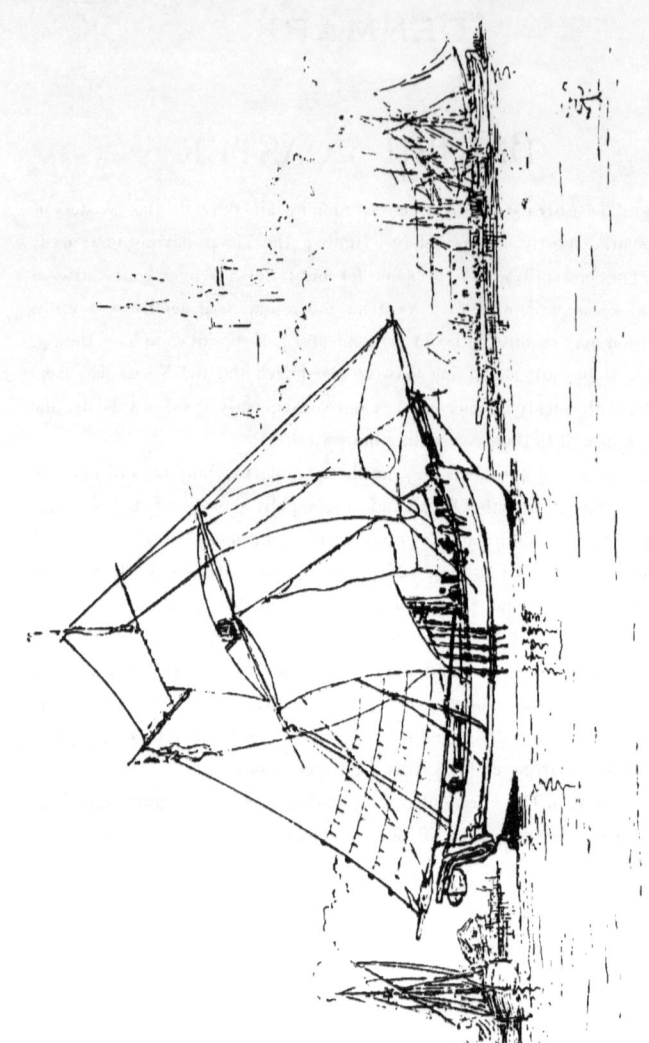

DANISH COASTER AT ROSKILDE

ground for them, and the city itself is very attractive to the archæologist, especially as the collection of Scandinavian antiquities, for which Professor Warsaae did such good work, is unrivalled. Thanks for this are due to the preserving qualities of the peat beds, in which have been found all the spoils of war buried to the honour of their gods, after their pagan manner. Even the wood work has been preserved in the form of chariot wheels, textiles also; and of course the bronze implements are in a perfect state of preservation. The twin-spired cathedral beyond our sloop is that of Roskilde, where the late Queen of Denmark was recently laid at rest.

HOLLAND.

ZOUT WATER SCHIP.

"A salt water ship" seems almost an anomaly for the description of a distinct class of trader. In Holland there is a particular industry of this kind still going on. The object is for the manufacture of salt, as extracted from sea water; and with such a boundless supply of material to work on, there surely should be no lack of salt anywhere. The Red Sea should be a good place for a zout water schip to go, were it not for the distance, for there the percentage of saline is very great, owing to the great evaporation.

These vessels are still fitted with big sprit-sails—a very favourite method with the Hollanders—a foresail and jib; the mast being a pole-mast carries no gaff topsail; the Dutchmen do not care much for cracking on, unless in cases of dire necessity.

No country has such a variety of rig and distinct class of traders as Holland. There is one particularly fine fishing boat hailing from Flushing, which is described in the notes on "Blankenberg" Brigs of Belgium.

"Hooker" is the general name for traders. Then there are hay vessels, "boot ships," "turf tjalks," pronounced "challocks"; fish hookers, to bring the herrings from the "buis" of Vlaardingen when at sea; the pinks von Scheveningen, "kof" ships, galliots, enkhuyzen.

"Buis" is a curious rig, rather like Norwegian jaegts, with one mast midships, carrying a big square-sail, with a small mizen to set when hove

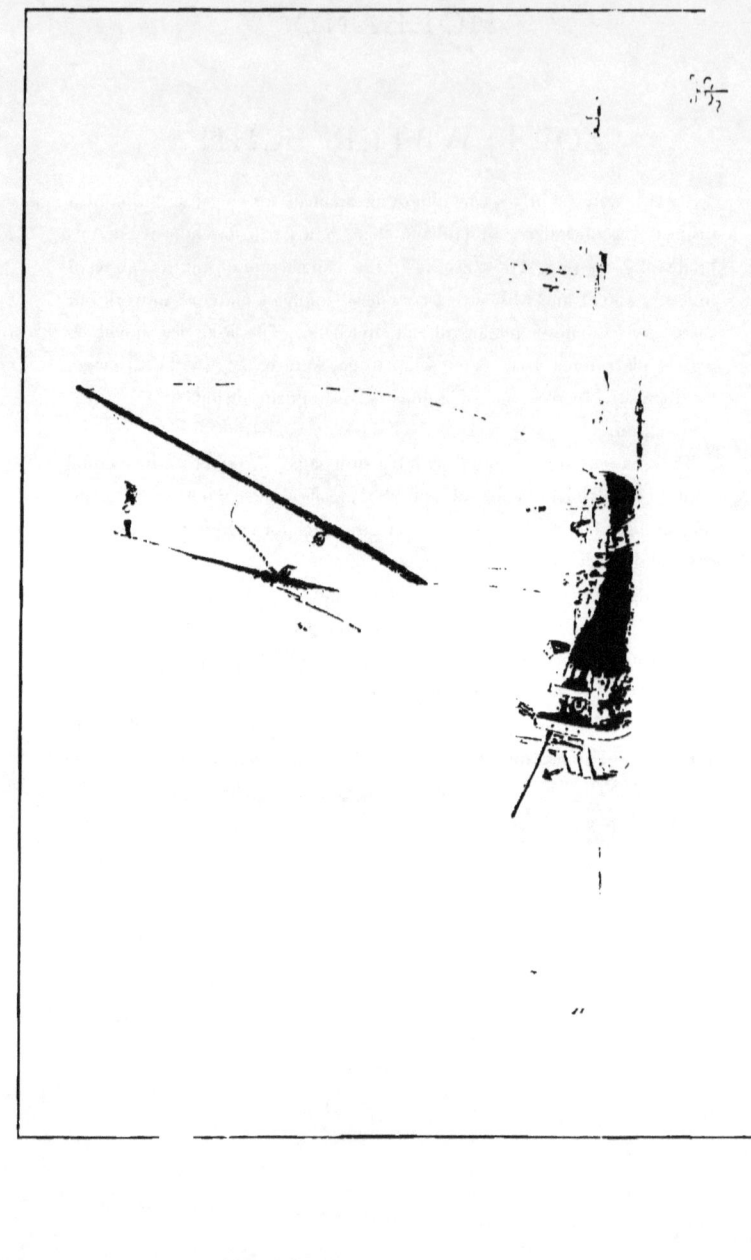

to, fishing. These are herring boats; they are also used for the cod fisheries, when they may be seen with their water sail anchors out to windward. "Smaks" are traders also; "poons" are smaller, as a passenger boat; "kraaks" are like barges with a short mast -long timber vessels; "hoeyers," small yachts, with a gaff sail and foresail, no bowsprit; "heynst," a small country market boat. "Sniks" are the same class larger; Friesland "praams," a small coaster, with every possible variety of ferry boat or "veerpont," with a large sprit-sail and jib, whilst on board may be seen a cart and horses, country chaises, ladies, gentlefolk, and country folk, all packed together. The Dutch are full of courtesy to those who visit their interesting country in a genial spirit, which is always a good traveller's companion and useful adjunct to the inevitable "Bædeker" or reliable "Murray."

HOLLAND.

DUTCH PINKS

THE Dutch have always been great on the great waters. How keenly we remember the names of De Ruytor and Van Tromp, and how successful were the commercial adventures to the Spice Islands, as shown by the Dutch Malay possessions in Java and the south part of Borneo, up to lat. 4 S. They were a great maritime people, and gave us a lesson, by which we have profited in every sense of the word. *Ex parvis magna:* from their small beginnings in the east we have taken up the running, and have done great things. Their East Indiamen traders were fine vessels; they showed us what a navy could do. We have followed their good example, and are much indebted to the brave little nation for the lead they gave us in days long gone by.

There are so many kind of craft in Holland that it is difficult to select one particular type. Perhaps the most familiar is a Dutch galliot, a vessel with ketch rig, that is the main-mast with gaff main-sail, flying square-sail, and top-sail stowed on top-sail yard, and in very settled weather a very narrow topgallant sail over that; stay-sail, jib, outer jib, and flying jib complete the head sail, whilst the mizen has just a high gaff-sail. These craft were the traders and general conveyances for passengers between Holland and this country before the introduction of steamers. In the Thames galliots were familiar from the days of our youth, and lately some built of steel have appeared, so now the Dutch are taking a lead from us. Let us say, " Imitation is next akin to flattery."

The next class well known, particularly to observant passengers, either going over London Bridge, or passing down the river, is that of the Dutch eel schuyts, which lie off Billingsgate, and have had that privilege ever since the Spanish Armada, 1588, " as heretofore accustomed "—a quotation from the Archives of the City of London. Their build has not altered in any way since that time. Three must always be there for the

SCHEVENINGEN : A DUTCH PINK COMING IN.

supply of eels to London town, and no vessels are allowed to moor or bring up inside them on the north side. Greatly to the credit of these good Hollanders, no case is known of any of them being up for misconduct during the many years the schuyts have been coming, for four centuries indeed. These craft are most typical, with a bent flag-staff rising from the back of the rudder; pole-mast with the conventional Dutch whiff; curved gaff, the bluff bows half hidden by fenders, eel baskets, and technical paraphernalia; and, most characteristic of all, on each side the sweerds, or lee boards of the old form, the same as in the days of Vandevelde.

Next akin to these schuyts, which come from Zealand in the north part of the Zyder Zee, are the Scheveningen herring boats, called "pinks." Their dimensions, like the laws of the Medes and Persians, alter not. Length 40 ft., beam 20 ft., depth 12 ft. Some years ago, when the builder at Scheveningen was asked if he always built to those dimensions, he said, "Yes, always. Would you believe, sir, that a man came to me wanting me to build him a pink 40 ft. by 19 ft.?" "19 ft! No, sir, you are foppish, you must go," answered the builder, and the new order was declined. From the great interest taken, the builder wanted to know if we thought of running a matscapay to build pinks in London; if so he would like one share, but they must be true, 40 ft. by 20 ft. beam, or he would not invest.

The rig of these boats is very simple, leaving them for the most part on an even keel. In very fine weather they carry a narrow topsail, called a "Mars" sail, which does not come lower than the head of the fore stay. The hulls are picturesquely painted with a scroll pattern on the weather boards forward; the head of the "sweerd" or leeboard is ornamented with some geometrical pattern; the heads of the mast yard are painted various colours, the whole topped by a gay vane when they start, and only a very frayed bit of bunting when they return. These craft have no bulwark or gunwale to protect the crew in bad weather, the wash-boards forward being considered sufficient. Being flat on the floor, they come on the sand of the beach, as directed by the flagman, sail set; and once they touch they settle down, with the sea breaking over them in the most unconcerned way, and wait for the ebb tide to leave them high and dry. In the winter they are hauled right up on shore. The herring carts are the same old build as the pinks, with very high backs. Each cart will hold seven thousand herrings, is painted green, and is drawn by three horses abreast. The boats, the carts, and the costume of Scheveningen women form a most picturesque *tout ensemble*.

HELIGOLAND.

HELIGOLAND (Anglice), Helgoland (German) is an island at the entrance of the Eider, which has of late absorbed the attention of yachting men and the yachting world, especially in the month of June.

On the occasion of her Majesty's Diamond Jubilee, 1897, the German Emperor announced that a cup of the value of £500 would be given by his Majesty to be competed for by English yachts over 50 tons, the time allowances to be according to the Royal Yacht Squadron rules: course, Dover to Heligoland, about 300 miles. Perfect arrangements were made to welcome the English visitors, who were to be towed up after the race through the canal to Kiel to join there in the Segelregatten des Kaiserlichen Yacht Clubs at Kiel. The whole thing was a great success, and so satisfactory to his Imperial Majesty that again in 1898 a similar prize was given and more yachts entered, amongst them the new schooner yacht "Rainbow," 317 tons. Although the race was only open to cruisers to sail in cruising trim, the "Rainbow" was to all intents and purposes a racing schooner, with 12,600 square feet of canvas, a lead keel of about 110 tons, drawing 17 ft. of water. "Caress," being a forty rater, could not be accepted. "Charmian," a recent schooner by Fay, was entered 175 tons. Then "Latona," 175 tons, was a likely vessel to get the much coveted prize in a long stretch of sea-way like the present course, one condition being to keep outside all lightships on the German and Dutch coasts. One schooner represented the old order of things, the "Egret," built in about 1858. One entered, but a non-starter, which should have done well had there been a heavy blow, was the "Goddess," true Brixham trawler type but larger, being 176 tons T.M., or Thames measurement, instead of the usual tonnage, 60. She was originally built for Mr. Schenley, and now is numbered in the fleet of Mr. F. W. L. Popham.

Eight yachts started from the Admiralty Pier at two p.m., all getting away well together, with a four-knot tide under them and a grand breeze behind them, some of the yachts carrying flying square-sails. The last seen of them from Dover Pier was that "Rainbow" had a fine lead and those aboard her were probably feeling rather confident of receiving the

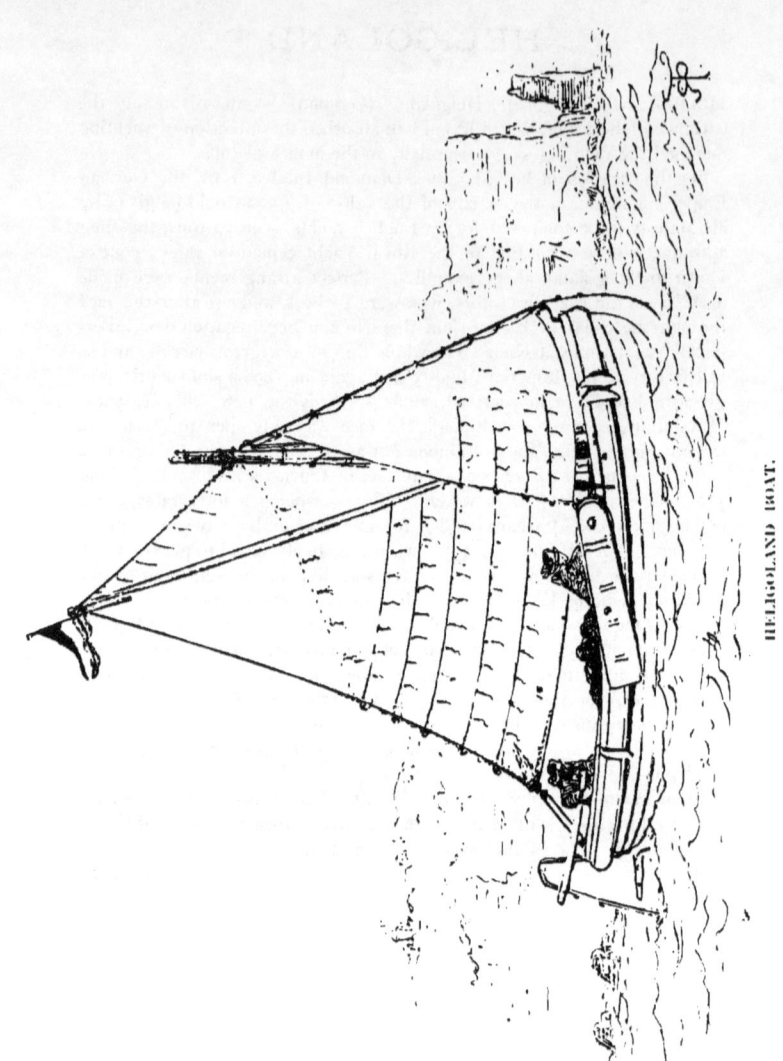

HELIGOLAND BOAT.

cup from the hands of the German Emperor. The finish was to be between the German man-of-war "Mars" and the black buoy with ball on staff on the south side of Heligoland. The distance of 320 miles was run by "Rainbow" in 24 hours and 15 minutes, arriving the following day at 2.12 p.m. off Heligoland. This, however, was not enough ; those alarming time allowances were anxiously awaited ; it was a long suspense, for she had to allow " Merry Thought," a yawl of 73 tons T.M., belonging to Mr. Cecil Quentin, 10 hours, and she saved her time.

When they arrived the German Emperor was there on board the Imperial white " Hohenzollern," a leviathan of a yacht of very imposing appearance, well known at Cowes, still looking like a cruiser, for which she was originally intended. The English yachts were towed through the canal, passing Rendsburg, and soon the Marine Akademie at Kiel resounded with the English tongue, which is spoken by all German naval officers, to the great convenience of English yachtsmen generally.

Heligoland looms like a huge old red stone block of cliff, is much frequented by navigatory birds, and must be a perfect paradise for the ornithologist if he could only persuade these visitors to stay a little longer. The island is now a German watering-place, where bathing is encouraged by a fine sandbank island some distance off the town, which appears to be the only place where a landing can be effected. The local craft give the idea of being specially intended to meet anything in the way of bad weather ; the reefs in the main-sail running half way up the leech, and five in number. These look like bad weather. Then a balance reef runs up at an angle of 45° from the cringle of the fifth reef. These balance reefs are still to be seen in this country in some fishing smacks ; they were used in yachting in the early days of Thames racing. Our alarm is eased down by seeing only four reefs in the fore-sail. Still, these precautions are the result of long experience and are good admonitions to new comers.

1899, June 19.--The Kaiser's gold cup was given in honour of the Queen's 80th birthday, the course and general arrangements being the same as on previous occasions. The " Charmian " schooner won.

BELGIUM.

BLANKENBURG BRIGS.

The sailor-man will naturally be somewhat surprised to see such a name attached to such a lug-rigged craft as this; but when it is explained that that is the local name for her all will be well. Coming out of the Scheldt from Flushing, when abreast of the West Hinder lightship several of these fishermen were in sight, and passing close to one, the pilot turning round to me, pointed, saying, "There, sir, that's a real Blankenburg brig." When pilots are taken on board to impart useful knowledge as guides, councillors, and friends, it would be uncourteous to contradict them, particularly as an explanation followed shortly after that they had two masts like brigs, only the square sails were sideways. Were it not a generally acknowledged term, the good pilot might have been maligned by our taking him for a sea-dog wag. The short foremast leaning over the stem is an eccentricity found in other parts of the world; it is shown in the "Bahia" river craft later on, where reference will be made to the lovely spot they frequent, namely, the beautiful Reconcava of Bahia.

Blankenburg is the favourite seaside resort of Belgians, who find Ostende a little too much and too noisy for them. It is no rest to visit a spot by the sea where all is competition for notoriety; staring advertisements mural and human, paining one's eyesight; extortionate charges; noise and glare, destroying repose of mind and body. To enjoy the seaside one must seek the peaceful comfort it offers when accepted in a simple way, with the blessing of renewed vigour and health.

On the shore opposite to Blankenburg, at the notable little fortified town of Flushing, is a very unusual combination of pilotage talent. The Scheldt divides Holland from Belgium; and as the main channel favours Flushing by passing nearer to it than to Belgium, an admirable arrangement has been made, whereby the Dutch and Belgians have both their stations most favourably placed at Flushing. The good-natured rivalry is very keen. Directly a sail is in sight both get ready and away they go, oars, canvas, or

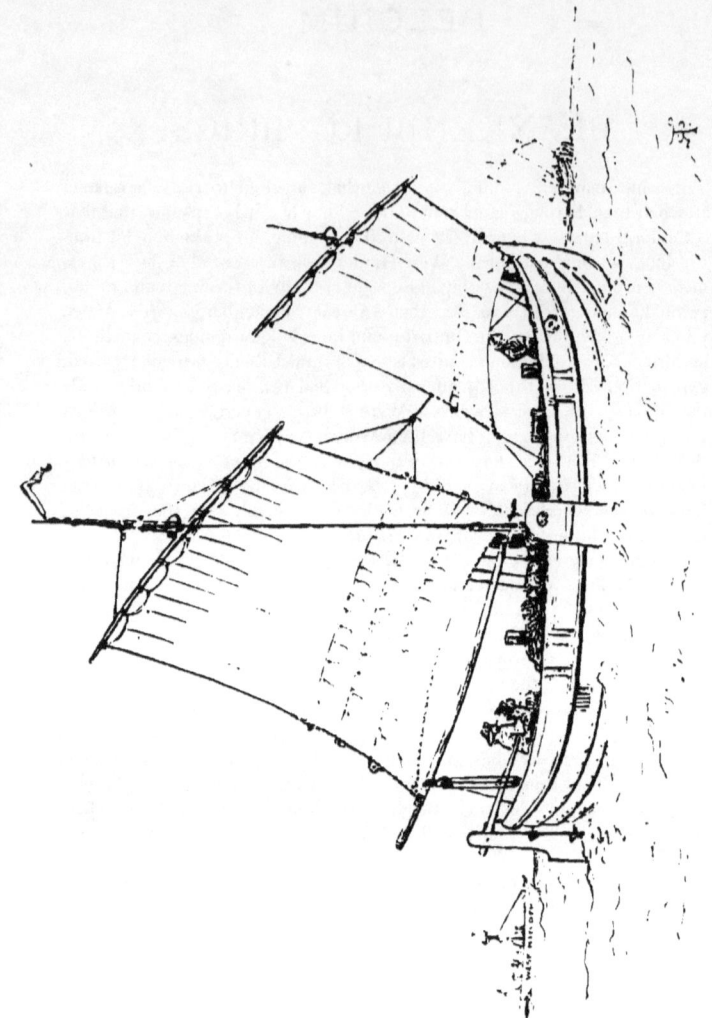

BLANKENBURG BRIG.

anything to get them along, whilst the struggle for mastery is anxiously watched from the shore, where the inhabitants naturally come down to encourage their compatriots, relations, and friends. This applies principally to sailing craft, as the steamers generally carry their own pilots. Outside there are again other members of the pilot family, here in the open, snugly getting about under easy canvas, with an unmistakable pilot flag flying at the masthead.

Round the " Wielinger " lightship and the " West Hinder " lightship, which is three hours out from Flushing by mail steamer, the Channel tides sweep down with great force; and should there be a strong wind from the N.W. the water is driven up the Scheldt, sometimes with disastrous result, the long line of rush being shown by a continuous line of white frothy scum. The entrance to the Scheldt is well lighted; but the lightships are small, much lighter altogether than those on our coasts, and constructed of steel, which must make them cold in winter and hot in summer for the poor fellows on board. Those on board lightships have time to notice these little items of everyday life so much more than any one employed at high pressure.

Now a farewell word to the " Blankenburg brigs!" They are very like the Dutch pinks just described; but, as the pilot remarked, they have two masts. Then the brigs are not decked boats, and the sails are very small; the "sweerd," or leeboard, is very narrow and dropped on both sides vertically; the bridle on the luff of the mainsail should not escape notice. The Flushing fishing boats are finer craft altogether, larger, and of better workmanship; in fact, a very powerful class, of great seaworthiness, such that we could take up to the Baltic. The Dutch are very proud of their " schokkers "—that being the name by which Hollanders distinguish them —so much so that a Dutch gentleman had one built as a yacht and visited Cowes in August, 1897. She has great accommodation, and must be a fine sea boat, with her bold high bow. Her length is 78 ft., her beam 22 ft. with 5 ft. draught. She has a polemast, and is built as a model to encourage yachting in Holland, which is a great compliment to my old friends the " schokkers." My humble friends, " The Blankenburg brigs," although they have two masts like brigs, with the square sails sideways, will never meet with such patronage.

FRANCE.

CHASSE-MARÉES.

The national craft of the west coast of France is certainly the chasse-marée, a name which is wonderfully twisted by our fishermen, and Anglicised until it can hardly be recognised without harking back to the original name for the sequel. For instance, some call them "slash-marées"; others, to be more English, know them only as "Charles Marys." One of these vessels is generally to be seen during the summer months lying off Southampton, trading from Morlaix in Brittany with onions. The crew, with their broad-brimmed velvet-bound felt hats, combine the commercial with the maritime, and persevere from house to house until their cargo is sold. The greater part of the fleet, however, is occupied in fishing.

Off Boulogne at one of the Channel races we had a curious sight, a big chasse-marée pounding along between "Iverna" and "Valkyrie," two of our most beautiful yachts; they were not long together. The dingy, bluff-bowed lugger was a great contrast to the snow-white, well-trimmed canvas of our racers, whose racing flags were neatness itself, whilst the Frenchman ran up an enormous tricolour, for they love a big flag. The chasse-marée is a big three-masted lugger, with a huge transverse crutch before the mizenmast, so that the mainmast can be lowered on to it when fishing. Three lugs and a jib is their usual canvas, with an occasional outer jib, as many of them have a jibboom. Havre de Grace is a great port for them, Boulogne having a large share of those fishermen, who work the English Channel.

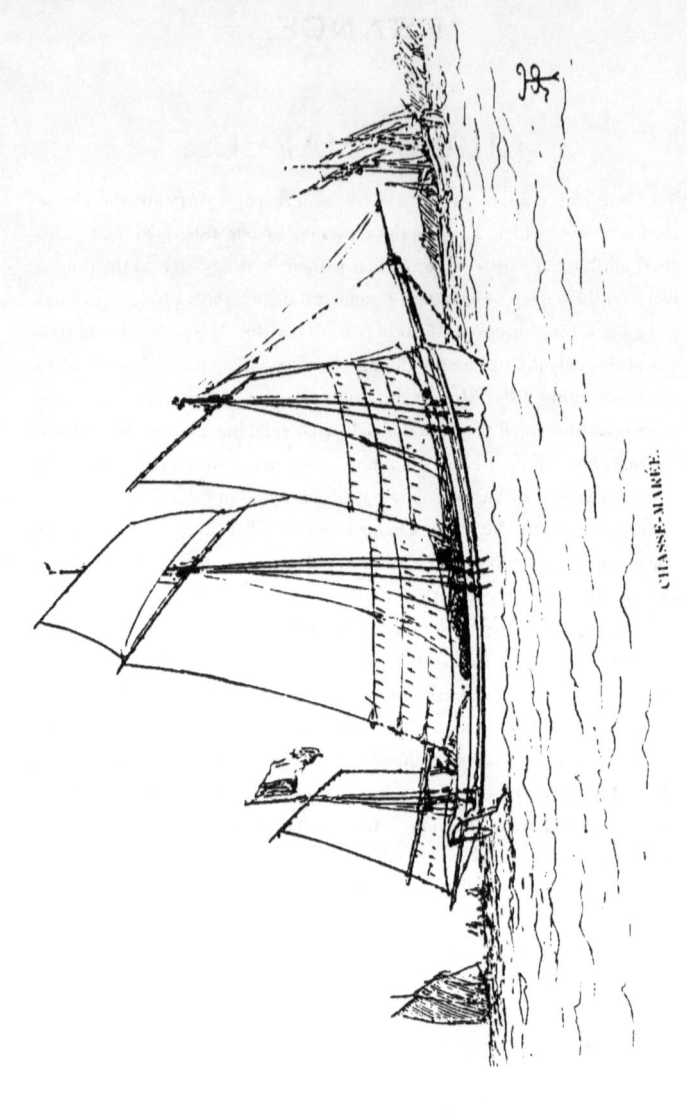

CHASSE-MARÉE.

It is from Havre and Bordeaux that the Newfoundland fishermen start for the season on the Bank, having in the French colony the islands of S. Pierre and Miquelon as their centre. These islands were ceded to the French as shelters for their fishermen, with certain conditions as to fortifications and garrisons, at the time of the Treaty of Paris. For the Newfoundland cod fishery the French use schooners. The annual take of fish is gigantic, although the seasons vary in productiveness ; still, the average is maintained in spite of an occasional " short catch," for the codfish is of rather a migratory turn of mind, and there are no signs of a failure of species.

PORTUGAL.

MOLETA FISHING CRAFT.

WE now come to lateen sails, or a main lateen, in the fishing-boats which sail out of the Tagus for the sea fish round the "Burlings," a group of rocks lying off the Portuguese coast shortly before rounding for the Bar of the Tagus. These craft are the very quaintest-looking things imaginable. Their black hulls; the piercing eye, reminding us of junks in China; the curious stem with huge spikes supposed to carry creels of fish, placed there to keep them next door to their native element; then the canvas, the names and number of which are legion. Even water sails are there, and the tremendous jigger, like the lowered mainmast of a chasse-marée, run out aft. The Penzance fishing luggers have powerful jiggers, much the same as Manx fishing-boats, but these are much larger.

These craft are called in Portuguese moletas. The principal sail is the big lateen; then forward comes a stay-sail from the mast-head to the extreme point of the stem, over that the jib from the mast to the bowsprit, and a lower water sail under the bowsprit like our old men-of-war of the seventeenth century. On the end of a lean-forward spar or foremast are carried an upper water sail and an outer jib. Now we must go aft to inspect the sails there. The main lateen comes down with two sheets; from its peak the aft canvas comes down sheeted to the end of the jigger; first a large fore-and-aft spinnaker, an upper spinnaker, and a third to fill up the open space above the end of the jigger. But why so many sails? For this reason; the moletas are trawlers, and the small sails are called "balance sails," to regulate the speed when the trawl is down. These vessels are very curious in their midship section, which in form is like an inverted Cupid's bow, approaching the shape of a double boat; in fact, very much like the section of a Seychelle double cocoanut, with the bottom of the keel not quite so low as the floor of the two sides. Off the "Burlings,"

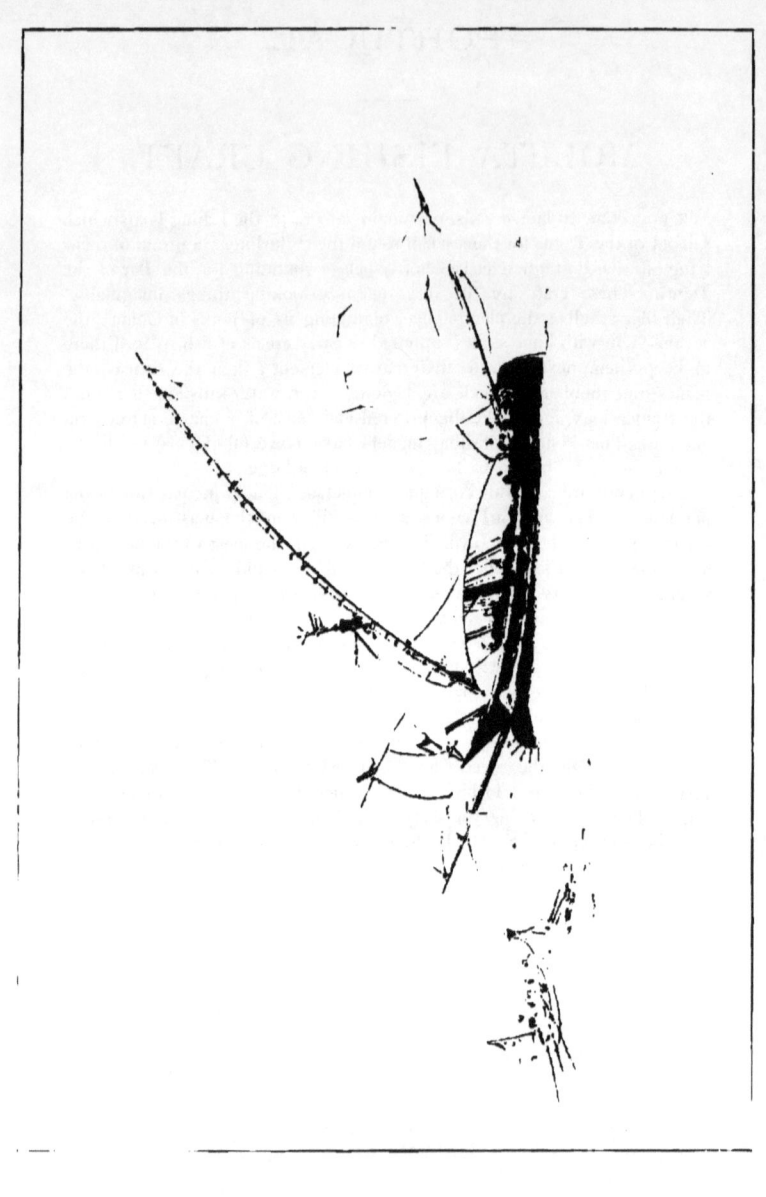

their cruising ground, is the place to study them in everyday life, and under their endless arrangement of canvas.

Over the head sails of the moleta rises before us the Castle of Penha, crowning the wooded heights of Cintra, that lovely spot, where camelias whiten the forest with their abundant blossom. Ahead of the fishing craft we see St. Julien fort, with a peep of Cascaes Bay, where much bathing goes on.

The official barge to the left in the illustration is a Custom House boat, with the Portuguese beak bow surmounted by a huge knob. Nor is this the only peculiarity. The national style of rowing is suited to photography, as at the end of each stroke the crew come to a dead pause, very pronounced, and this is the moment for the camera to seize its victim. The crew pull another stroke, so that the pace is not killing, but slow and dignified, as becomes officialdom.

SPAIN.

SPANISH CRAFT.

THE inland sea of the Mediterranean affords a great variety of rigs, lateen sails predominating, whilst its meteorology is eminently capricious; what with dead calms; the mistrals, which whip the sticks out of yachts if not smartly handled; the Levanters, which sweep down from the Rock at Gibraltar with such force that there is a standing order that no small boats going off are to carry canvas. It is the Adriatic squalls that necessitate a special rig for coasting craft called "polacca" rig, so that the whole canvas can be lowered at once and sent down with a run, without any mastheads in the way, although these vessels are brig-rig. Then there is also the dead heavy Campsine wind, which is familiar to most people who have visited the Holy Land. Fortunately typhoons, monsoons, and cyclones are confined to distant lands; but mistrals are frequent.

To meet these various pressures of wind power many devices are used, most craft being prepared with long sweeps for dead calms, when the canvas will not draw. These considerations certainly impress one with the great advantages of steam power, whereby such regularity of progress is secured, with one great advantage, that steaming in a dead calm, say twelve knots, it is delightful to go forward and feel a comparatively refreshing breeze instead of oppressive baking heat under an unventilated awning.

The old feluccas or Maltese galleys must have been splendidly workmanlike looking craft, with the high poop of the early period of the sixteenth century; the poop, with its big lanterns emblazoned with the rich

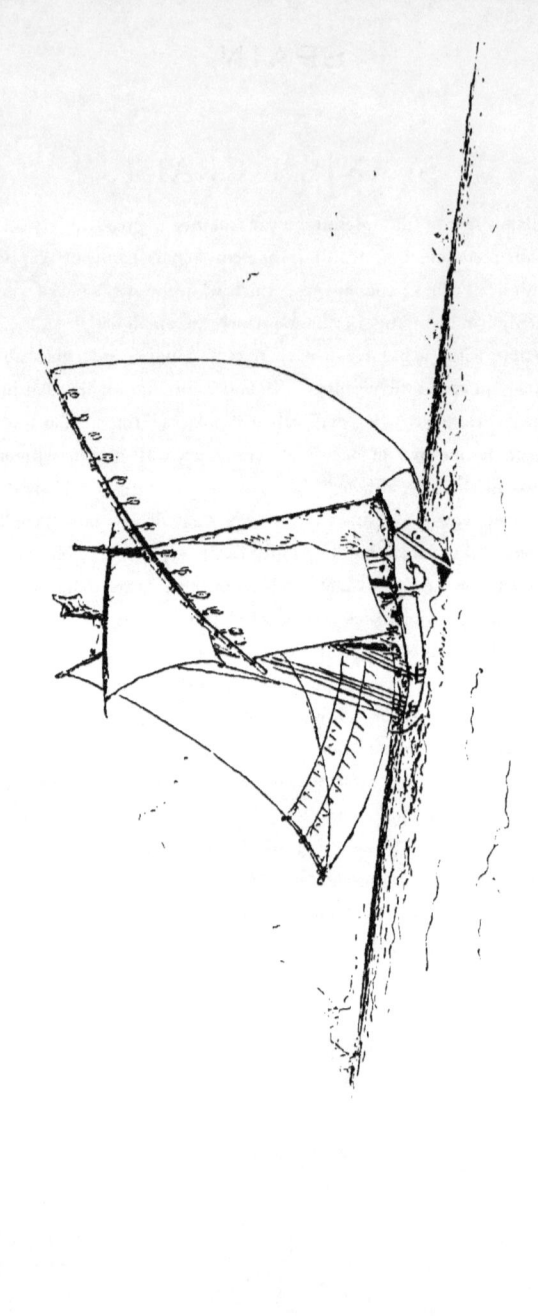

costumes of the Knights of Malta; the three huge lateens wafting the deep red hull through the blue waters, the forty-four scarlet sweeps doing good service to increase her speed, as each sweep had three stalwart rowers. Imagine the change from this bright and exhilarating scene to a heavy mistral off Galita Island, when the modern auxiliary schooner-yacht is hove-to in a gale, with her topmasts housed, the result of careful study of the yachtsman's best friend, the barometer.

Such incidents of the Mediterranean and experiences of many kinds probably led to the Spanish rig of the coaster shown in the illustration. The gaff mainsail may be considered an intrusion in the Mediterranean; but, reefed down, would be a comfort in bad weather, with her head sails snug. Naturally sailors who all their lives have been accustomed to lateens can handle them to the best advantage, but even when brailed up they are very unwieldly in a seaway, and very long.

BARBARY.

ALGERINE CRAFT.

DIRECTLY the Strait of Gibraltar is past then comes the home of the pirate, that blood-curdling word, which brings up visions of melodramatic sea-ruffians of evil purpose, picturesque in colour, bristling with weapons, and diabolical, perhaps murderous, intentions. Of course mail steamers are safe enough, their speed soon leaves the good old-fashioned pirate a long way astern; the steam yacht can do likewise. The beautiful white-canvased yacht caught in a dead calm, her sails reflected so distinctly that it is difficult to discriminate between the reflection and the reality, that is what the pirates pray for.

It seems absurd at the present day to mention such a thing, but after passing the Rock there is a hornets' nest to the southward; for who has not heard of the Riff pirates? And beyond the Riff coast is the Algerine pirate, and to the northward after passing Gibraltar the coast of Spain fascinates the yachtsman as he sees the lovely sundown tinging the snows of the Sierra Nevada. Beware! There, on this side, is the Spanish pirate, the marine *contrabandista*. Even as late as 1894 he went for an English lady's yacht off Cartagena. The Earl of Cavan in one of his delightful Mediterranean books relates how on arriving at Vathy in Ithaca, one of the Ionian Isles, he found the "Sirex," an English yacht, lying there, and when the "Sirex" party came on board the "Roseneath," Lord Cavan's auxiliary screw schooner, they gave a very graphic account of their escape from pirates off Cartagena. The breeze came just in time to waft them away out of the horrible grasp of the Spanish buccaneers. On the south side one of our crack racers returning from the Riviera got becalmed and threatened. What a temptation to the wily Arabs to see 11,000 sq. ft. of lily white canvas! But the breeze came and the "Ailsa" gracefully bade them adieu. Inside the Rock take the advice of the naval officer to Lord

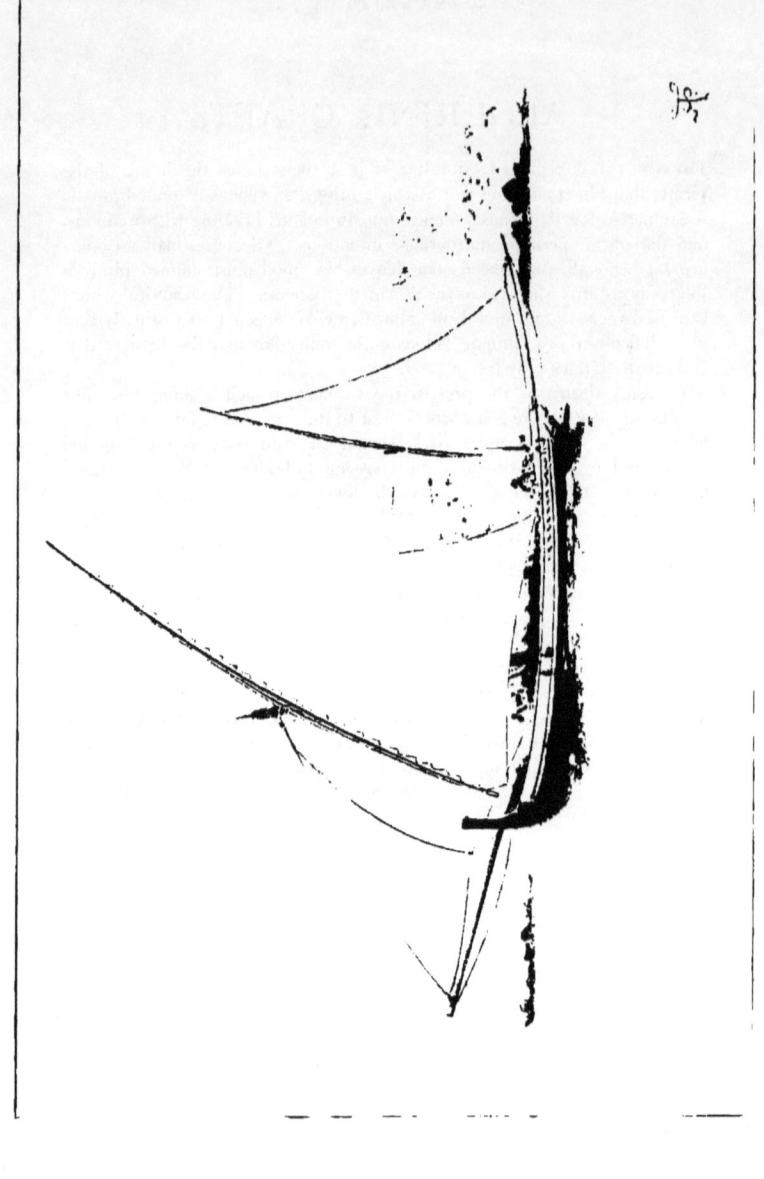

Cavan: "Along the coast of Riff and the coast of Spain be wise and go armed!"

Two kinds of lateen craft used to be spoken of in the Mediterranean as feluccas and xebecs, the former generally associated with Spanish, as in the term Spanish "Felucca." The "xebecs" were principally referred to in Algerine piratical proceedings, for which sport the three-masted large lateen-sailed craft, with numerous and powerful sweeps, were well adapted. Doubtless as we improved our yachts, building them for speed, so these nefarious gentlemen gradually got the hulls with finer lines and more sail spread, using their big jibs as spinnakers.

There is something very romantic about the high peak of a big sail of this form, and when they are cracking on goosewinged, every stitch of canvas pulling hard, flying through the blue waters, leaving a roaring, foaming wake, it is a sight to be seen and not forgotten.

Our Algerine vessel is a respectable member of the coasting trade at the present time, probably carrying goods to Gibraltar, finding commercial pursuits steadier and more regular in returns than the excitement of piratical raids interlarded with periods of downright laziness, which the climate tends to encourage. The high stem in this vessel is of the same character as the Portuguese, which gets straighter till quite vertical at Naples and Messina, and down the Italian coast.

ITALY.

VENETIAN FISHING-BOATS.

VENICE must have been magnificent in the sixteenth century, particularly towards the end, when the genius of such painters as Titian, Paul Veronese, and Tintoretto flourished. What a grand sight the gorgeous ceremony of wedding the Adriatic Sea must have been, a ceremony instituted in gratitude for the vast benefits she had conferred on the Venetian commerce and navy in the twelfth century, and one that increased in splendour and richness of colour as the wealth of the State developed. No wonder great painters were born in such an atmosphere of prosperity and cultivated tastes with such glorious surroundings. The old palaces and great canals still give some idea of what Venice must have been in the zenith of her glory, surrounded and nurtured by the riches of the whole world.

Some idea of the richness of the local colour is handed down to us in the sails of the Bargozzi fishing-boats still existant. Take, for instance, the mainsail in the boat of the illustration. The peak in the upper part in the original is red, with a pale yellow crescent in the centre. At the base of this colour is a fine curved line of yellow, next a band of red, then a line of white, terminating in squares of red on the alternate cloths of the canvas. On the white central part of the mainsail St. George and the Dragon are boldly emblasoned in an oval. The upper line of reef points is bright red with red squares, like battlements in the alternate cloths pointing upwards in line to those at the base of the peak decoration. Under the upper reef line runs one of rich deep yellow, then inverted battlement pattern of same colour leaving white interstices. The second reef line towards the foot of the sail is of a lighter yellow, with mauve-coloured squares in line with the red ones, following the same cloths. The foot of the sail is a fine weather-beaten mauve colour. The colour in the foresail harmonises, but is less elaborate in ornamentation. Some sails are deeper in tone but richer in colour, with vandyke browns, madders, deep

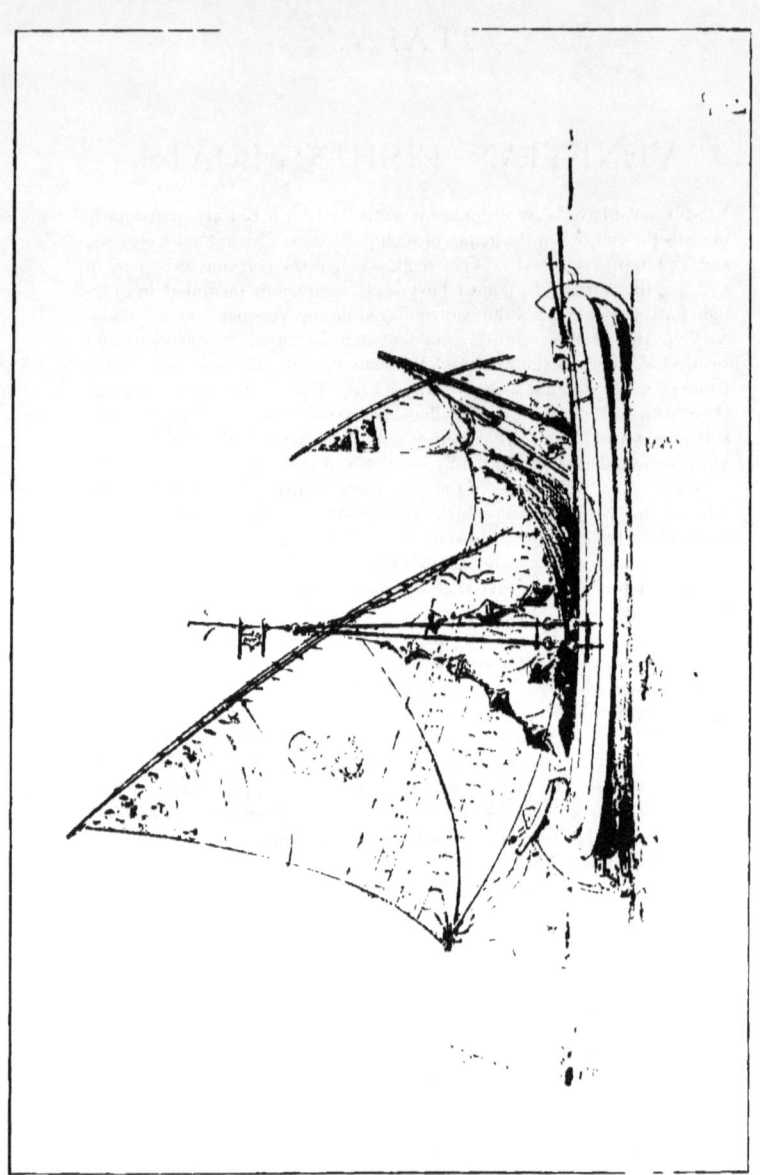

BRAGOZZI—VENETIAN FISHING-BOATS.

blues, orange chromes, burnt siennas, and purples blended and weather-worn, to the grandest blends of luscious colour. The hulls are not very symmetrical ; in fact, one would have expected finer lines and bolder form when we think of the grandeur of the State barges of the Doges, those long life potentates who were in vogue and power for eleven hundred years.

Venice still retains one very prominent feature, the "gondola," the graceful gondola, the aquatic Venus of Venice, lovely in form and most romantic in association, strongly associated with soft moonlight, soft music, and lovely women, paddled by stalwart gondoliers in gay garments, yet the gondolas themselves are so sombre. In the sixteenth century it became compulsory to paint them all black. They have remained so ever since ; in fact, one cannot imagine these "water conveyances," as Evelyn called them when he saw them, of any other colour. They seem hardly to touch the water, so beautiful are their lines, and are propelled by one gondolier generally, two being the exception. The oar is of considerable length and purchase, of 13 ft., resting on a very curiously devised 21-in. crutch, which is always on the starboard side when the single gondolier is in his usual position aft. The whole length of this dainty craft is 36 ft., beam, 4 ft. 5 in. A little abaft midships is the cabin or house for passengers, which is about 6 ft. and height 5 ft., the sides leaning inwards, the roof ornamented with black knobs of silk. The stem-head is like a Roman galley, bow rising much above the house, made of thin polished steel and serrated forward, the stern terminating in a beautiful specimen of steel work.

TURKEY AND EGYPT.

SMYRNA CRAFT.

BEARING up to the northward we soon find that we are getting away from the lateen waters, and at Smyrna meet a new acquaintance of a very different type. This vessel has a mast of the same length as the enormous large sprit by which the mainsail is supported, the end of the sprit being held by a very strong stay from the masthead, where the standing rigging and shrouds terminate. This strong stay acts as a curtain-rod, along which the sail is run out on rings, so that in India it would be a "purdah" mainsail or curtain-sail, for such it is. The vessel has a bold sweep of high and sudden sheer forward, with a bowsprit which "steeves" like an old man-of-war's. A large staysail comes down on the bowsprit outboard, with outer and flying jibs beyond. The square canvas consists of large flying foresail and topsail over it, both being set on very long yards; at the stern is a rather large deckhouse, with a large green flag with a crescent. All the way up the Archipelago through the Dardanelles to Constantinople these vessels will be met or overtaken.

The curtain arrangement strikes an English yachtsman as very domestic, clumsy, and old womanish; still, "every man to his trade, sir!" The natives describe it as being so simple. When you wish to use it, you haul it out along the curtain-pole in this case a strong stay; and when you no longer want it you can haul in as much as is required, especially should a squall be imminent, and you are snugly canvased at once.

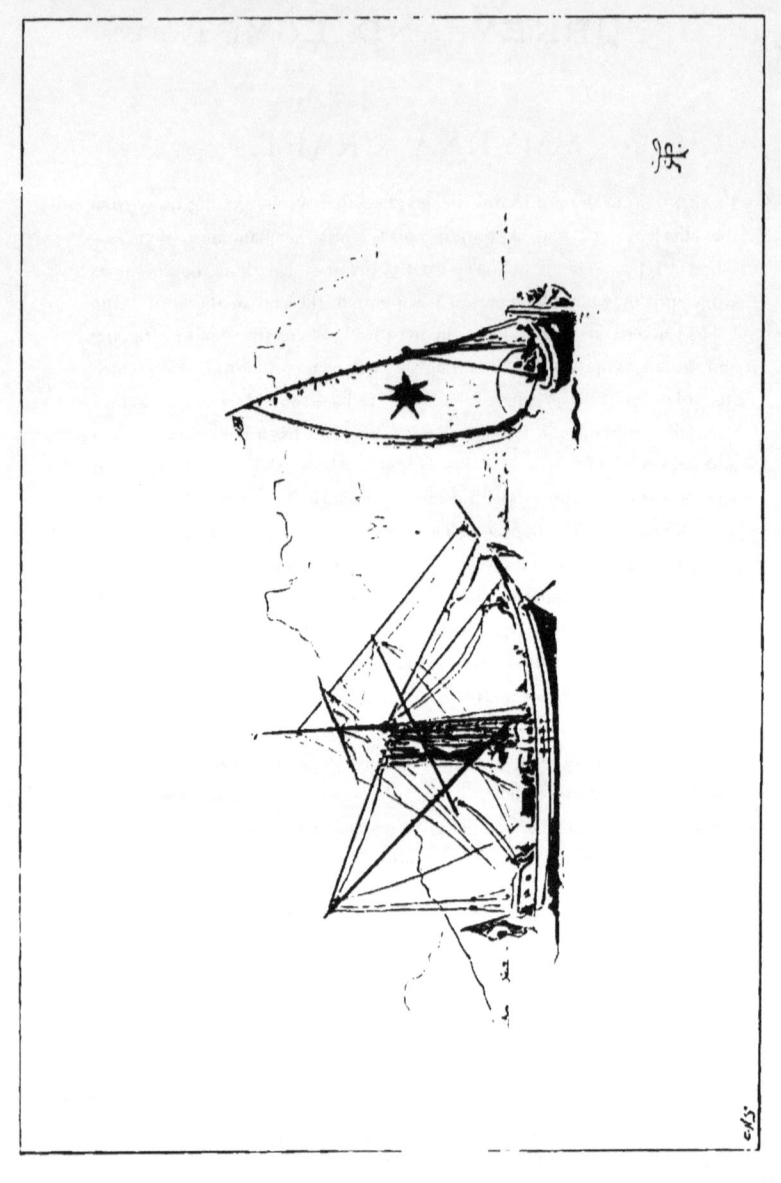

SMYRNA CRAFT.

Some lateen craft come up from the Mediterranean with merchandise. It cannot long be so, for the aggressive commercial tramp is on the war-path, and steam communication is increasing everywhere, we may say to the ends of the world, happily carrying the English language, or, at any rate, a Scotch engineer.

Smyrna is grandly situated, with a bold hill rising at the back, crowned by old fortifications. The harbour is good, with a fine quay, but the town requires some equivalent to Eau de Cologne unfortunately, so that on landing one of the first questions is, When do we get on board again, or go off?

TURKEY AND EGYPT.

CONSTANTINOPLE CAIQUE.

"EXPERIENTIA docet." at least so it ought. Directly a yacht approaches the Dardanelles the only way to save much trouble, anxiety, and annoyance, is to hoist a red ensign, that being the commercial flag that passes the boat comfortably. Still, the owner of a Royal Yacht Squadron vessel, after having been round the world, perhaps, must either do that or wait at Chanak until a firman arrives from the Sultan, and the Governor has the order to let him pass or no. White ensigns, the privilege of the R.Y.S., and the blue ensign as a Naval Reserve flag, are tabooed; and should either of these flags pass the forts of Chanak without the necessary permit, two blank shots are fired across their bow; should the hint not be taken, then the third is shot, and as one may suppose, the third one is not often required. Constantinople is more beautiful from without than from within. The Golden Horn is very striking, the picturesque boats flitting about with sturdy Turks rowing caiques, highly decorated State caiques, with drapery richly embroidered hanging over the gunwale of the stern sheets: all is fine in colour but a little solemn.

The Turks are, as a rule, a fine, sturdy race, as shown by their soldiers at Plevna, and not less by the rowers and boatmen generally in the Bosphorous. The oars have a special peculiarity. Inside the rowlock there is a balance of a large egg-shaped piece of wood, which the rowers consider a very great help, as taking off the weight of the length of oar outside the gunwale of the caique. The dress of the rowers is very dandy-like and showy: the voluminous baggy trousers or knickerbockers, very full indeed, generally dark blue: a crimson kummerbund or sash, and crimson tarboosh with blue tassel: a thin white shirt, over which is worn a Zouave jacket embroidered according to the station or dignity of the owner of the caique, who usually reclines rather than sits in the stern sheets, under some decorative awning. The more truly Eastern scene is when Youth and

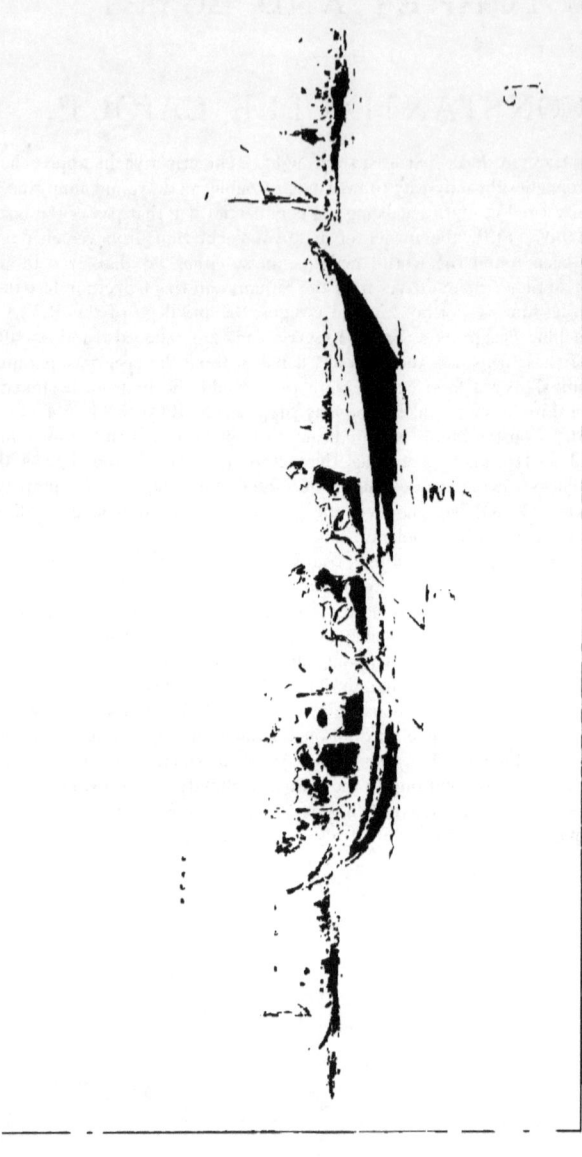

A CONSTANTINOPLE CAIQUE.

Beauty are seen reclining in gorgeous caiques, with light robes of diaphanous muslins richly embroidered, dainty slippers of marvellous workmanship and finish ; an air of lazy luxury pervades the whole picture, which is heightened by the remarkable contrast of a Nubian or Ethiopian attendant in gorgeous attire right aft.

The city of Constantinople presents an especially beautiful effect as the morning sun first catches the tops of the slender minarets, and, gradually descending, illumines the sleeping city. It is not, however, under these circumstances that the most impressive view is obtained, although the lovely delicate tints of the morn appeal to the artistic mind ; it is the approach to Constantinople by moonlight which most forcibly appeals to the poetical mind, and deep must be the impression made, for it is a scene which can never be effaced. Much has been written about the simple grandeur and soothing beauty of the Taj-Mahal at Agra, " the glory of the world," as the white marble is softly illuminated by a young moon, the full moon being almost too strong. Others again prefer the frowning grandeur of the Colosseum at Rome as seen by moonlight ; but beyond the beauty of these the approach to Constantinople on a moonlight night is impressive and beautiful, the reflections on the waters of the Bosphorus adding greatly to the charm of the scene, whilst the dark hulls of the shipping intensify the chiaroscuro with their long shadows and flickering reflections.

TURKEY AND EGYPT.

THE KHEDIVE'S "DAHABEAH."

So many visitors have been attracted to the Nile of late years that the most familiar name of passenger and pleasure boats is that of "dahabeah." As the visitors increased in numbers so did the number of luxuries obtainable on board these craft, till at last they had *tout ce qu'il fallait* and a little more. Although steam has made its mark from the delta of the Nile to Fashoda in various forms, and steam navigation been applied to war and peace purposes, it is gratifying to the lovers of canvas that the Khedive remains faithful to the old river favourite "the dahabeah" as a pleasure craft.

There is one feature very peculiar, and confined to the river Nile, about the way in which the huge yard of these boats is carried. Most lateen sails are hoisted so that the upper part of the mast is seen above the hoisting point on halyard blocks. In the Nile boats there is no part of the mast above the yard, which rests in a saddle on the mast head. To get that yard into that saddle does not seem an easy thing, and even when there to keep it there. The yard is fitted with two single halyards, one on each side of the yard, just below where the saddle would come. Each halyard passes through a single sheaved block on each side of the mast-head, so that when the yard is hoisted home it will be found in position, ready to be lowered into the saddle, to do which, check the tack and a very gentle pull at one of the upper brails or downhaul, and the yard is on active service in the saddle. The appearance to an Englishman is flat-headed and ugly. It seems to meet all the requirements of the inhabitants of those parts; nothing short of the general use of steam and abolition of lateen will terminate its career.

The precursor of the later dahabeah period was the sternwheeler steamer for the Upper Nile, built by Yarrow for shallow waters. Soon after the Khedive had a steam yacht the "Safa-el-Bahr," built by Messrs.

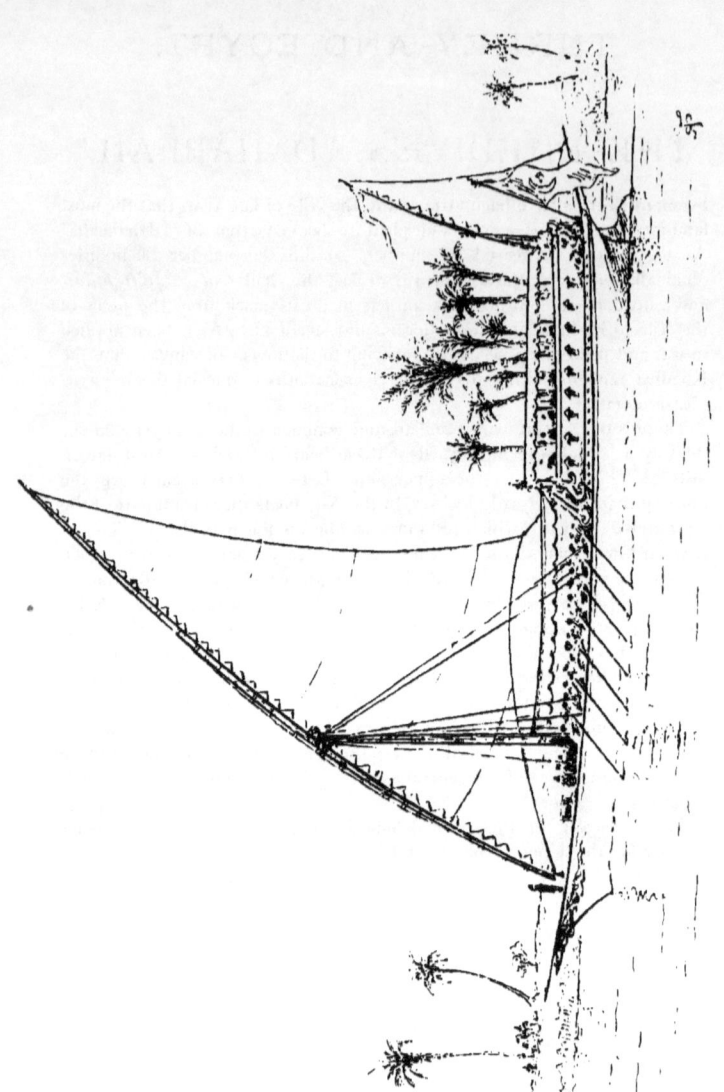

THE KHEDIVE'S DAHABEAH.

A. & J. Inglis, of Glasgow, a beautiful vesssel constructed of steel, schooner rig, with two decks for ventilation.

Her length	221 ft.
Beam	27 ft. 1 in.
Depth at side	17 ft. 3 in.
Draught	12 ft.

1,200 H.P. indicated.   Speed 14·1 knots per hour.
Tonnage, Thames measurement. 677 tons.

The dahabeah of the Khedive is certainly a very beautiful vessel, with fine lines, a very refined "nugger-de-luxe." Having two masts, she belongs to that class. The after-part is carefully constructed for every possible chance of ventilation, there being a large commodious cabin with poop, over which is stretched a double awning. Between the end of the cabin and the mast are the rowers, fourteen in number ; they too are protected by an awning stretched over them. The bow finishes very gracefully with a short bowsprit, which is more for ornament than use, there being no hoist for the jib with the Nile conformation of masthead. The dog-tooth finish to the end of each cloth is as usually seen in all lateen sails, whether in the Mediterranean, Red Sea, or Indian Ocean.

TURKEY AND EGYPT.

"NUGGERS" ON THE NILE.

"NUGGER" is the native name for Nile boats carrying two lateen sails, one very large on the foremast, the after one much smaller. They are the commercial river conveyances, and carry good cargoes. In these boats the stem rises up abruptly, probably as a precaution against the broken water knocked up by sand-storm squalls, which so suddenly burst over them. If such precaution be necessary, why should they carry lateen sails of such unproportionate height? Simply because they are required of that size for average weather, and when the unusual occurs their canvas is brailed and shortened with that rapidity which only experts can carry out under such trying circumstances.

These nuggers have been doing good service for us about Omdurman and Khartoum, especially in carrying grain; and in the construction of the railway they carried tons of iron rails for us. In these boats there is a short bowsprit, from which the light kedge or anchor is generally strung, with a sheet of the foresail to the end of the bowsprit, as the foremast is placed very far forward, most likely to allow more space for the cargo.

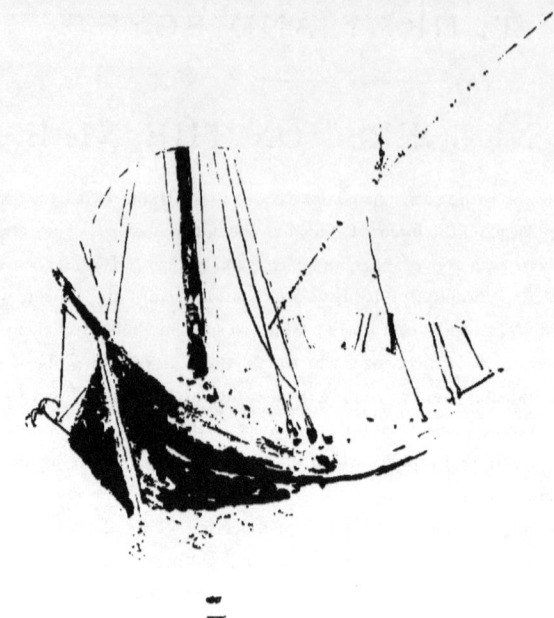

A NILE NUGGER.
Coming down with grain.

These boats were very useful to us, and the owners rejoiced in the justice and fair dealing meted out by the military visitors. It must have been a new life to them to have "plenty work and plenty," with too much or rather without any "backsheeshing." Doubtless the inertness of their previous life must have received rather a shock when first they were introduced to the work and energy of the campaigning of a British force, in full swing on the advance to a goal they were bent on reaching.

TURKEY AND EGYPT.

THE "GYASSI" NILE BOATS.

THIS native name is not known far from the banks of the Nile, as it is the local name for cargo and passenger boats on the upper part of that great river. Carrying only one enormous lateen sail, about the largest ever seen on a boat of her length of water-line, even with a lead keel of proportionate weight, the rapidity with which the crew will take in this large surface of canvas astonishes any watching the performance for the first time certainly.

The mast is about two thirds of the length of the water-line, and the yard twice the length of the mast, consequently the distance to the tack is the same as the peak of the sail is from the masthead. The boat itself is constructed in the most lumbering, rough way, resulting, nevertheless, in great strength, and the usual number of the crew, like French bread at a restaurant is *à discrétion*. The stays are thick and heavy, naturally, to support the tall mast and the large spread of canvas. The lofty lateen sail represents a very curious sight when it has to be furled, for instead of brailing up only, as the yard cannot be lowered, a very unusual sight is afforded by the sudden appearance of the hands "away aloft," lying out on

A NILE GYASSI.

the yard, even to the tapering peak end, to accomplish which a lad leads off, and after a few more lads of gradually increased weight, then come the men. The agility of Arabs is quite familiar to us in this country, from seeing the performances of Arab acrobats, who have from time to time favoured us with a visit. The function rather reminds one of "up the main rigging and riding down" the main halyards in a racing cutter here at home.

INDIAN OCEAN.

THE ARAB DHOW.

THE Arab dhow is widely spread and a splendid sea boat. In different localities it bears different names; for instance, at Bombay they are called "pattamars," then on the Coast of Cutch they become "buglas," and on the Indian Ocean coast generally "bugalla," or "baggalas" on the North-East coast of Africa. They are really the old traders, working between the Red Sea to the westward, and Bombay and the Indian coast to the eastward. They are powerful vessels, of some two hundred tons burden, mostly 85 ft. to 90 ft. in length, with a beam of one quarter of length, and would draw 13 ft. to 14 ft.

A dhow belongs to the "Nugger" family, but of a much finer growth; being a deep-sea trader, her stem is long and projecting, with a prow head or scrowl. This is technically called "grab built" when the cutwater is at an angle of 45° or 50° from the water-line; her mainmast is half her length overall, and the yard rather more than her full length. The mainmast leans towards the bow, at an angle of 80°; the hull has a fine bold sheer towards the bow. The mizen on the poop is about half the size of the mainsail, as far as one can judge at sea. The Arabs are very much given to a broad white line painted with a few ports like our sailing ships. There is no mistaking a dhow if the main halyard block is noticed, which comes down in a line with the keel—an enormous square block with four sheeves in it. When Arabs work they do work, and are very keen. Dhows do not carry a fixed bowsprit, using a jury mast or spar on an emergency.

There is another craft which in design reminds one much of what we have lately arrived at as the result of applied science. It is rather difficult to describe it without a diagram. Our last racing yachts in profile are tremendously cut away at the fore foot, and with a very raking stern post; the two lines if carried on would soon bisect each other. That is the

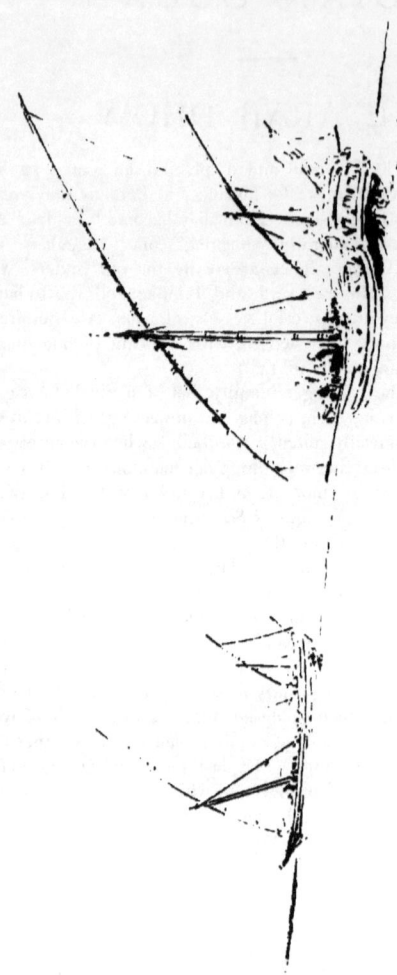

ARAB DHOWS

profile of this particular kind of dhow which used to be known as a
"batello," with about one third of the triangle cut off above the point
where the two lines meet. Another feature is that these craft have no
submerged rudder post, a balance rudder being fixed on a timber at the
stern above the water-line, and, coming down deep into the water, has
tremendous leverage. This timber for the rudder is like a rudder-post,
proposed by Mr. Read of Port Glasgow in 1873, and called the dog-legged
or angle stern-post by G. L. Watson in his admirable chapter in the
Badminton volume. Another point is that the deck plan of these craft is
quite like that of the old "America," having greatest beam a little abaft
the mainmast, but the dhow is much narrowed in at the taff-rail. Her
entrance lines are very fine, so the old Arabs had a keen idea long years
ago " of what the water liked " best to allow of high speed.

INDIAN OCEAN.

ARMED VESSEL IN PERSIAN GULF.

MODERN naval architecture has not penetrated far into this part of the world, and evidently the shipbuilders and ship-men cling religiously to the manners and customs which their forefathers have handed down to them with full instructions to be like the law of the Medes and Persians, which altereth not. Certainly this craft does not show any signs of having yielded to the flirtations of modern times and inventions. The Malays were great rovers, and this craft, although on the coast of the Persian Gulf, carries much Malay character with it. The double outside rudders almost remind us of the twin screws in home waters at the present day. Still, the dhow character predominates, with the two masts and high stern, more encrusted than the Mohammedan dhow, yet with a square transom; the mast-head is Malay in form, but the gong is not at all a Malay instrument of music.

The armament of this vessel must have shaken her pretty well if frequently discharged, unless the charges used were small and the powder weak—a safeguard often thoughtfully arranged by the purveyor.

Many years ago a fine trade was carried on from London and Birmingham in supplying "Bonny" muskets to the West Coast of Africa; they were curiosities in those days, say sixty years ago. The stocks of beech-wood with the comb of the butt uncut, were painted the brightest scarlet: the

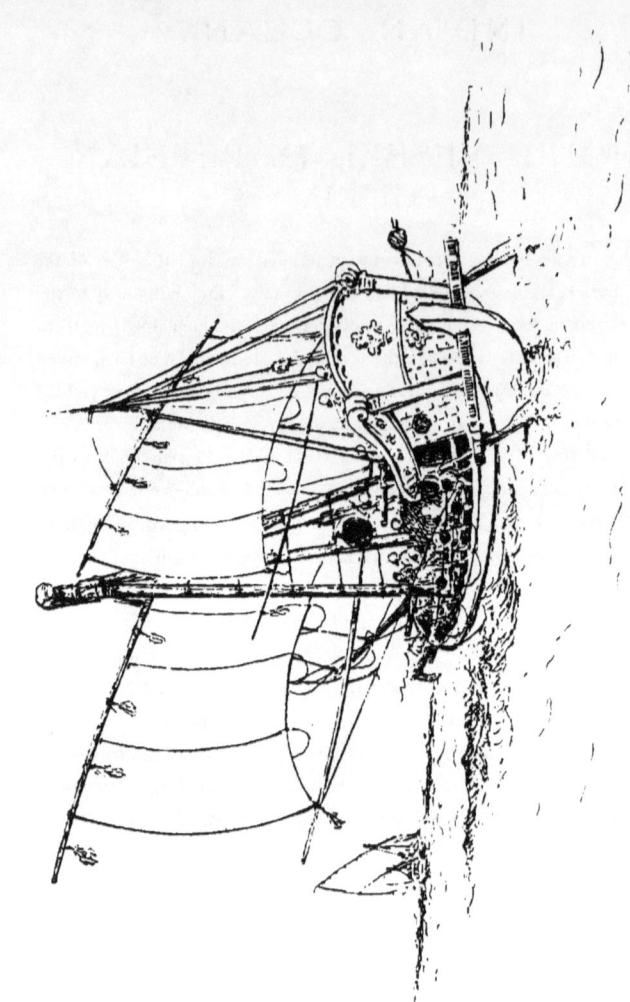

A PIRATE OF THE PERSIAN GULF.

barrels very long, with the scarlet-painted wood running up to the end of the long barrels, producing a very telling effect ; the locks were of an old flint pattern. Tradition says the price of these "articles *de vertu*" was seven shillings and sixpence. One of the merchants in Birmingham at that time was a Quaker, who on being remonstrated with for engaging in such business replied, " Friend, thee doth not know that *I* supply the powder."

INDIA AND CEYLON.

BOMBAY YACHTS.

THE Royal Bombay Yacht Club is an admirable organisation, favoured by a combination of circumstances which makes it quite unique in its social standing. Of course the first object was yachting, which was well taken up by the officers of both services and leading Europeans, producing a very good little fleet, composed of eleven lateen rigged yachts, three steam yachts, four schooners, four cutters, two yawls; the largest craft being the "Zingara" schooner of 268 tons.

The great race of the year is that of the lateen class, which under racing canvas look very large and above their real tonnage, requiring big crews. The starts are very exciting, and the manœuvring causes a mixed feeling of anxiety and merriment—anxiety on board the competing craft, the merriment principally amongst the spectators, who crowd down to the Apollo Bunder or Wellington landing stage, over which stands the very fine building of the Club House of the Royal Bombay Yacht Club, whose hospitality and welcome is well known and well remembered by all who have had the pleasure of receiving it.

The course at Bombay is not a long one, not more than twelve miles, so that the racers can be watched all through from the balcony of the Club, whence they start and whither they return. After leaving Quarantine buoy on the port hand, they pass South Carenjo black buoy with globe on starboard hand, rounding the mark boat off Gull Island, mark boat code flag W. on starboard hand, the Sunrock light and Dolphin lights to port, and

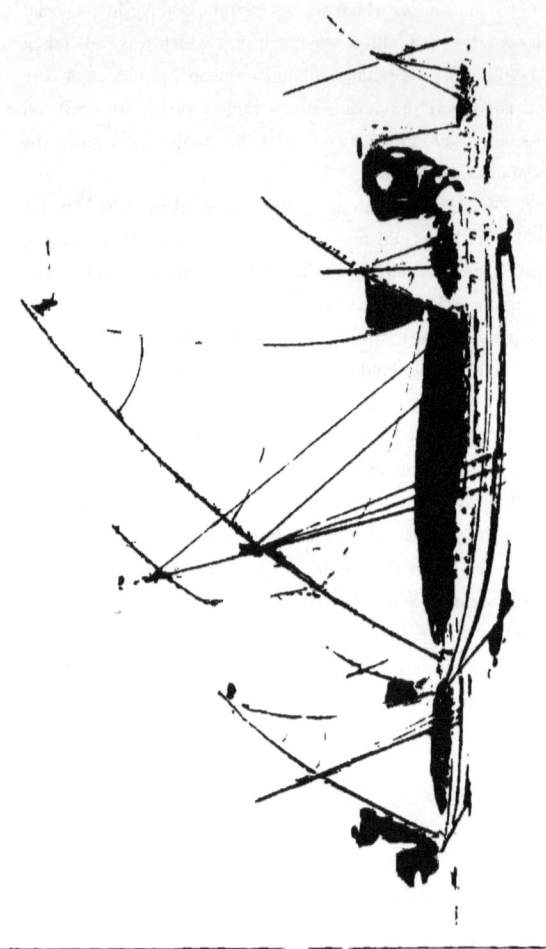

finish at the Apollo Bunder. The rules of the Y.R.A. have been adopted in all matters of regulations and time allowances, giving general satisfaction. Here it is very pleasant to find how the enjoyment of yacht racing is enhanced by having no protests, no professional jealousies. They sail for the pleasure and fun of the sport, and the spectators enjoy it in the same spirit. Jib topsails are supposed to be spar destroyers. In these waters the novel adjunct of a topsail over the big lateen sometimes brings trouble and disaster even to a turn-turtle function, which is " caviare" to the multitude on shore.

INDIA AND CEYLON.

CEYLON OUTRIGGERS.

No class of boat has ever been more popularised by a large circulation of small models than these Colombo fishermen's craft, which, although really an outrigged narrow hull, are mostly called " catamaran." A true catamaran has no gunwale. The catamaran of Bahia in Brazil, composed of round timbers, usually three on either side of the central long piece, has no gunwale. Again, in others at Madras and on the China coast the bamboos are all awash. We find this is the case on all surf coasts.

The Colombo craft have oddly-shaped hulls, the midship being very globose, suddenly falling in to form a gunwale, so that a relation is at once created with the deck plan of an iceboat, which is a trough. The outrigger is very large and strong braced, so large that were it a little bigger these craft would be in the category of double-hulled boats. They are not heavily canvased, carrying a very moderate-sized spritsail, set in a peculiar way; the tack is brought down to the bow, the bamboo mast equidistant from stem and stern, about the length of the hull on the water-line, the sprit always resting at the foot of the mast. The huge outrigger is always on the starboard hand, supported by two very powerful outrigger lateral bumpkins. It is a fine sight to see these craft running for the harbour at the break of the S.W. monsoon, their tanned sails pulling hard, sheets taut like Æolian harp strings, the bamboo masts curving to the force of the blast; sometimes only a part of a sail may be seen, the crew and hull being hidden in the trough of the sea. Beyond is the great breakwater of Colombo, engineered by Sir John Coode, defying the strength of the great combers as they bound in, sending them off at different angles in cumuli of spray and spindrift. Within the breakwater all is peace and calm; fishing boats hauled up on the beach, the picturesque natives grouping in bright colours on the yellow sand, which harmonises with their rich dark complexions and coal black hair. The background of this picture is quite

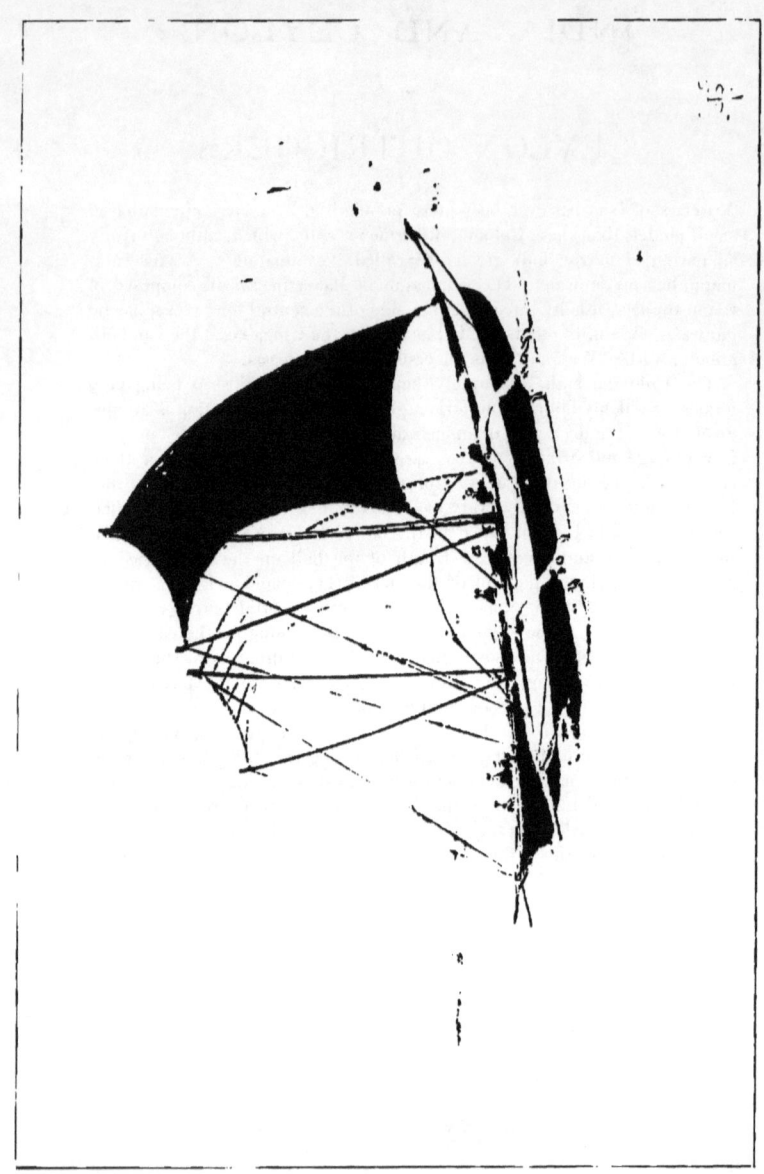

OUTRIGGER FISHING-BOATS, COLOMBO.

Cingalese, the untidy but useful cocoa-nut trees growing down to the water edge, backed by dense jungle such as Sir Samuel Baker loved when he described his experiences in his wild sport book of "The Rifle and the Hound" in Ceylon.

The fauna and flora of Ceylon have an immense range, from wild elephants in the former, and in the latter to the magnificent "Talipot" palm when in flower as the last grand flicker of vegetable life, for thus its grandeur culminates in beauty at its death. A visit to Kandy shows the wonders of this botanical paradise, for wild elephant sport can only be obtained at its best farther north.

INDIA AND CEYLON.

CINGALESE COASTING VESSEL.

THIS vessel, when I pictured her, was lying in Colombo harbour, a perfect blaze of colour in the strong sunlight. She was painted red, and the reflection in the water was beautiful and bright, the whole toned down by the dense vegetation on shore in the background. She was a true Mohammedan, from the decoration round her gunwale, backed by the appearance of the crew on board.

The dhow character is shown by the main-halyard block, which always looks so unwieldy, whilst the anchors are stowed in the bows, after the Chinese manner, but the mizen has a touch of European method about it by being a gaff sail and not a lateen like the mainsail; the standing bowsprit is also another feature, evidently suggesting an extra jib in favourable weather. A still greater innovation occurs in the presence of the outrigger to port; truly in ships and coasters we find strange mixtures of neighbouring countries most incongruously mixed up in the same craft. In this vessel we had a fine entrance with a counter and stern full and round like the "billyboys" on the east coast of England.

Another point is very noticeable—that the mast-head tapers and curves forward, like a Dutch pink coming to a point. Whatever her private life may have been, the sketch faithfully shows her external appearance as she lay in the harbour of Colombo, and the description given there was that she

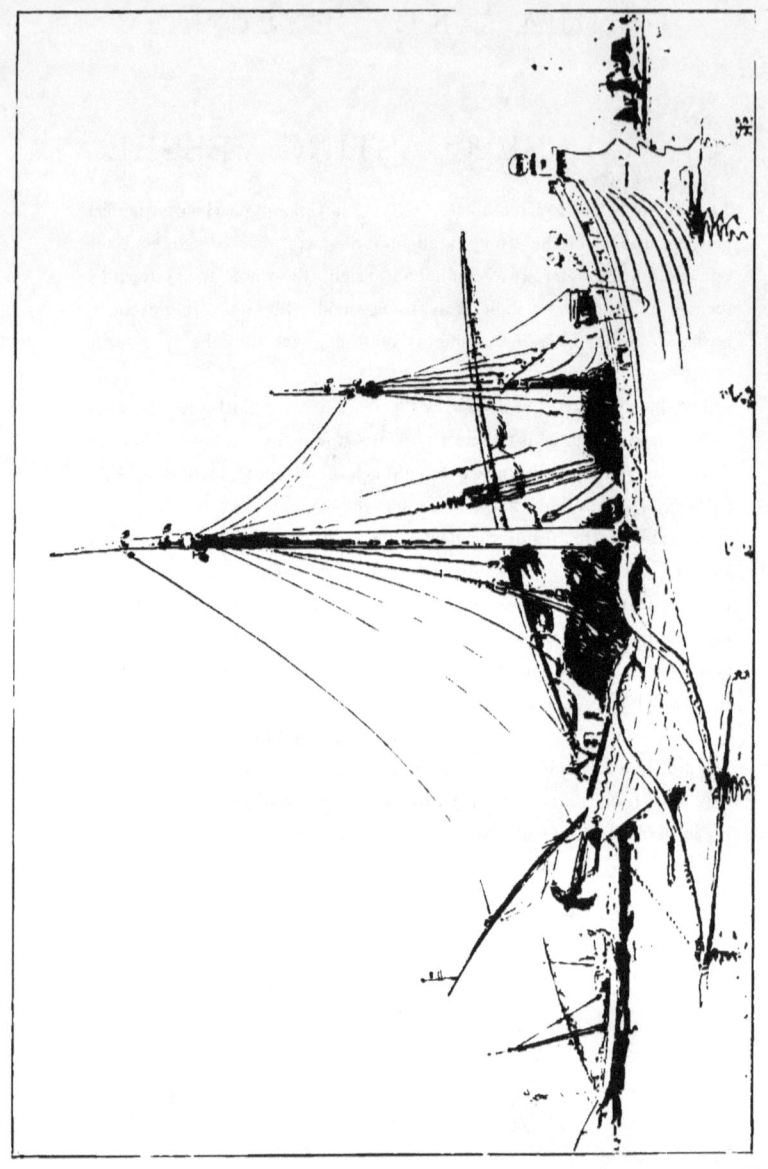

COLOMBO COASTER.

was a trading coaster. The thatch covering may have been put up temporarily to protect the crew whilst in the harbour from the sun's perpendicular rays, which in Ceylon are as powerful as anywhere in the tropics, only tempered by the wise provision of the universal sea breeze. It is the friend of the traveller as well as of the native, who gets so accustomed to its regularity, that when referred to by any one visiting, he only remarks, "All right," which explains everything.

BURMAH.

BURMESE RICE BOATS.

THE rice boat of Burmah is a very striking object, and once seen not likely to be forgotten, with its huge curved yard bent like a bow, high sweeping stern, and swelling canvas, all under the command and will of the high-throned potentate at the tiller. This arrangement of rudder strikes the uninitiated as unwieldy and clumsy, but leverage is wanted, with power, and they both are practically obtained.

There seems to be one great advantage in the navigation of the Irrawady productive of ease and comfort to all availing themselves of its facilities. It is simply that the prevailing winds carry the craft with merchandise up the river, and on the return journey the stream brings them down, having the one resort to fall back upon, namely, to anchor till the weather moderates.

The first glance at these craft makes us think how useless they must be on a close reach. The double mast gives great strength, but for such light canvas it seems hardly necessary. The great sheer of the hull seems to herald the approach of the Chinese junk architecture. The entrance of these craft is very fine indeed. When in cargo the freeboard is very limited, whilst the high stern seems enough to turn the vessel over. The Burmese cannot do without little flags at all points, at the mast-head, even at the yard arms, and at the stern. In this again we notice a Chinese influence, *via* Mandalay, most likely.

Some of the canvas is set in a very curious way, so that when they wish to reduce it there is no reefing; instead of doing that, every alternate cloth, or as many as may be necessary, is taken out, giving a very droll appearance, so that there are vertical strips of alternate sail cloth and landscape. Again, to our European ideas it seems such a very left-handed

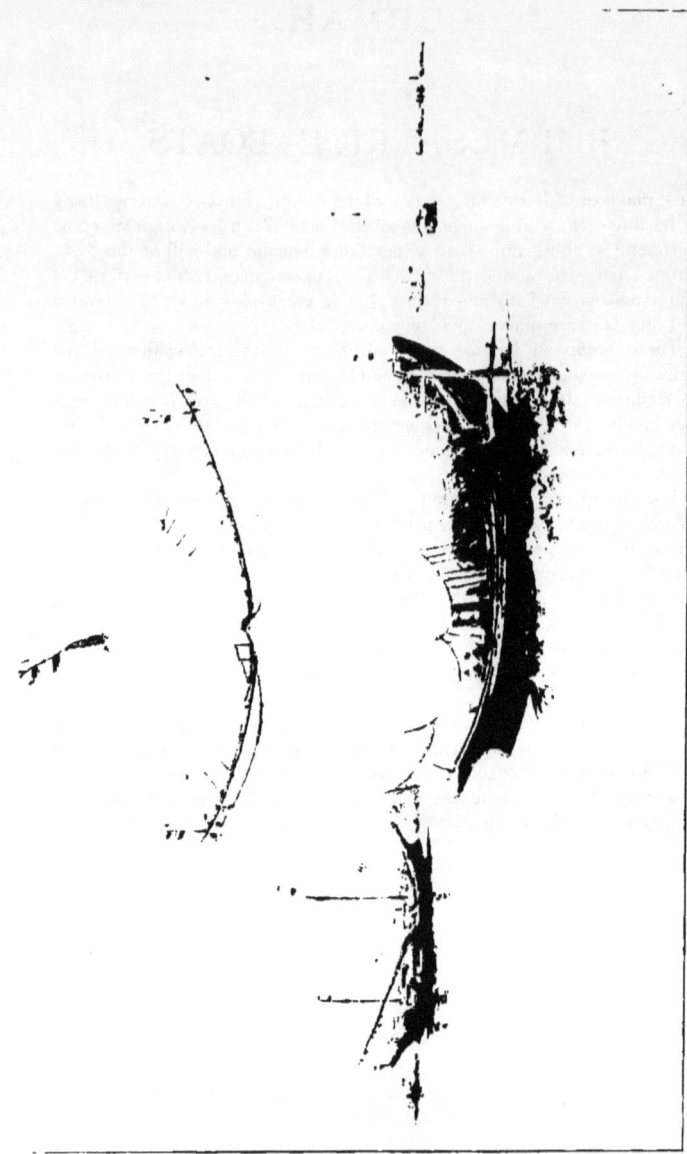

RICE BOAT ON THE IRRAWADDY RIVER.

arrangement to have the rudder on the port hand some feet away from the side of the vessel, instead of being in a line with the keel. They consider that their system gives greater purchase, so we bow, retire, and say, *Sic sit.*

The North of Burmah is the great teak district, producing large supplies, which we hope will be kept up by careful forestry, a science of great importance in a case like this, where Nature, bountiful as she is, is likely to be worked out, strained by the constant demand on her production.

The vessel on the left-hand middle distance is an upper river rice boat, known by the native name of "Hnau," with three masts and eight paddles —a much lighter craft than that with the curved yard and heavy stern.

BURMAH.

RIVER BOATS, RANGOON.

THE approach to Rangoon, situated on a branch of the Irrawady known as the Rangoon river, at once impresses the traveller with a vivid idea of Burmah. Rangoon has of late risen rapidly into importance, and now is blessed with public buildings, hospitals, and lovely gardens, principally the result of a great trade in rice. The true Burmese character of the town remains unchanged, the people equally picturesque, the natives just as fond of a choice flower coquettishly placed on one side of their shining black hair, and the pagodas with bells and little gilt crowns are still being erected regardless of cost, whilst the great pagoda Shway Dagohn rears his proud and gilded head to nearly the height of 400 ft. Around it is clustered a dense forest of minor and still more elaborate pagodas, the tenants of this forest being innumerable Buddhist priests clothed in yellow. The entrance is guarded by two immense stone monsters with open mouths, tusks, and teeth; these are supposed to deter the evil spirits from intruding on such holy ground. In 1852 the Irrawady river was blockaded by Captain Lambert, and Rangoon was captured by the English under General Godwin in the month of May of that year.

Teak and rice are the features of commerce on the Irrawady, which runs up country for a thousand miles. Teak, which used to be so valuable for our teak-built East Indiamen, has now been applied to so many other uses that its importance and value is still maintained; besides, this prophet is well appreciated in his own country, for all the river boats are constructed of it. The Rangoon elephants, which are leading features in the lumber yards where the timber is stored, evince an intelligence in moving the huge blocks of teak only exceeded by their docility. They not only move a log but stack it, first lifting one end up on to the pile, then going to the other end to push it up to the balance, and then to its final position. Now

RIVER BOATS, RANGOON.

all this is taught by kindness; there is no "unca" or steel prod in the hand of the mahout or driver; a little touch with his heel is quite enough to steer the huge animal, who understands his work and does it. In one part of the yards the logs have to be placed on a platform to be run up to the circular saws to plank. As the elephant pushes the mass on the platform, he will just step back to be sure that it is going straight and square. Heredity is a factor, as it is found that in the elephant family a good father and mother have good sons and daughters to follow on. One thing has to be remembered about these intelligent creatures—they never forgive if their attendant gives them short measure or offends them.

The boats on the river are most beautiful in their lines and curves, yet with all that, strong and well balanced. The very fine, thin counter or stern can hardly be accounted for, except for the beauty of line. The row boats have this as their special feature, the sterns of the larger craft being much higher. Then their ornamentation is quaint; no colour catches the eye on the boat itself; the beauty of colour is centred in the garments and headgear of those on board. They are fond of peacocks as an ornament, and the steersman is always in a state chair of elaborate carving, whilst his deep-toned complexion is usually protected by a kind of Japanese parasol. Fortunately in this warm climate of lat. 17 N. the tiller does not require either much exertion or much locomotion; it is an exalted position, combined in most cases with repose.

Here the Chinese sampan is now generally adopted as a sort of knockabout dinghey, with its swallow-winged stern, the rower always standing with his face to the bow.

BURMAH.

MOULMEIN SAMPANS.

MOULMEIN is the next important town to Rangoon in Burmah, lying a short distance from Rangoon to the south-west. The city is finely situated on rising ground on the banks of the River Salwen, an important river running far up into the teak country, which accounts for the great trade carried on in this valuable timber. There again we find our intelligent friends the elephants hard at work as at Rangoon. It is a new view to take of animal creation to look upon quadrupeds as labour-saving machines, which these elephants really are, when we see the heavy work they do and how they think of the work in which they are engaged, stepping back to see if their work is straight and square. The foreman particularly mentioned that they are most earnest at their regular routine, more than when put on just to exhibit their power before visitors, because in that case they are not sure what the next function will be.

The population here seemed to contain a great many Chinese, who had imported their favourite and national water conveyance, the sampan, as at Rangoon, whilst the natives keep to their beautiful light river boats, with a small thatched cover midships, formed like small models of the Burmese boats in the rice trade, which have been referred to as "hnaus." The bright and rich colours of the river folk blending splendidly with the dark colour of the teak of which the hulls are constructed, fortunately innocent of misplaced coats of paint. The picturesqueness of these groups of boats

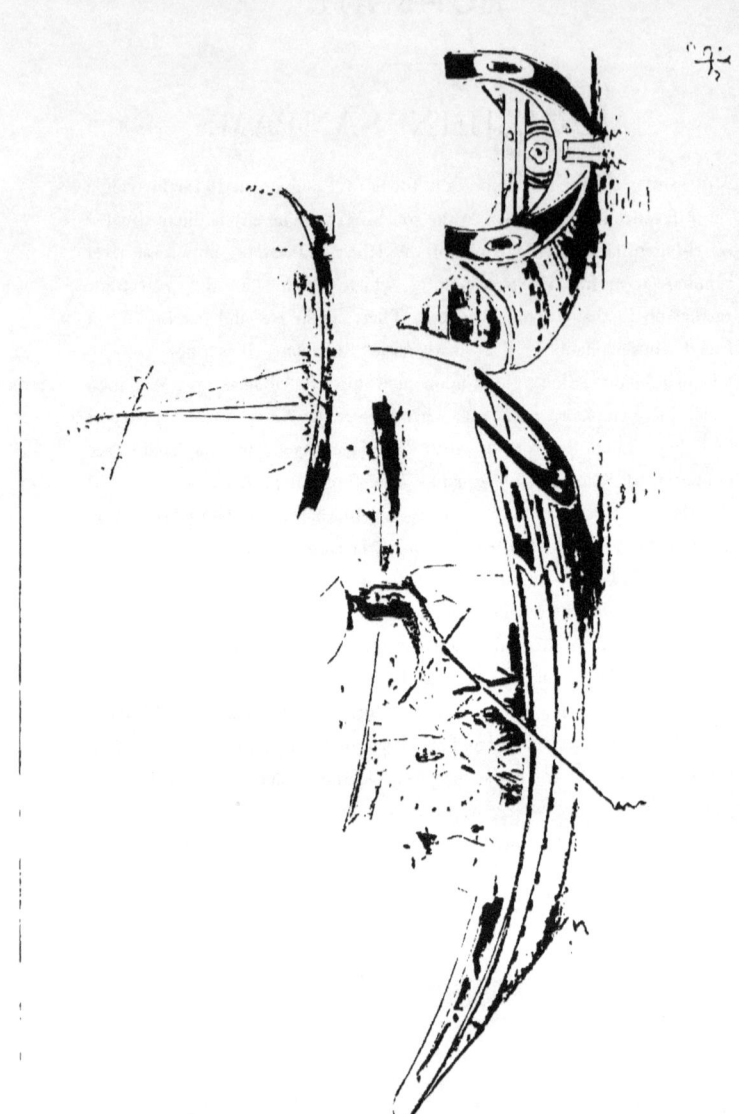

SAMPANS AT MOULMEIN, BURMAH.

is much enhanced by the way in which they are moored ; not having arrived at the useful little kedge, they content themselves with the ever-present bamboo, which is stuck into the sand for a mooring, and these lines or poles break up the repeated forms of the gunwales of the boats when clustered together —the whole crowned by the indispensable little Burmese flags and weathercocks.

THE STRAITS SETTLEMENTS.

SINGAPORE.

HERE we arrive at a Chinese influence which pervades everything. Pigtails everywhere, whilst the offing presents a spectacle of special interest, namely the great lumbering Chinese junks which come down with the north-east monsoon from Tien-sien with produce from the north of China, and then wait at Singapore for the south-west monsoon to waft them back again. Surely they must be the last of a race of commercial coasting giants, and steam will wipe them out very shortly. The monsoon arrangements were convenient for the pirates of Formosa and the Chinese coast generally, as affording a well defined season biennially for their sport, about the same time as March and October brewing in the good old houses in England. One of these huge Tien-sien monsters came over to this country for the Great Exhibition of 1851, and lay in the West India Docks. The marvel was that she ever got here.

The Island of Singapore is the centre of the Straits Settlements, forming a very important and prosperous Crown colony, with a delightful climate, which is blessed with showers of rain such as can hardly be expected when we remember that Singapore is in lat. 1° N. The regular cool wind at night is always refreshing after the heat of the day. The city is very cosmopolitan in appearance, from the curious assortment of Chinese josshouses, Hindu temples, Mohammedan mosques, and government buildings, yet with all that there is a prevailing stamp of British energy and prosperity on all sides.

The immense extent of wharfage at once stamps it as a centre of English commerce, and the whole is crowned by the White Ensign flying on the top range from the signal station, and with the Union Flag over the fort. Sir Stamford Raffles was the founder of this important colony about 1820,

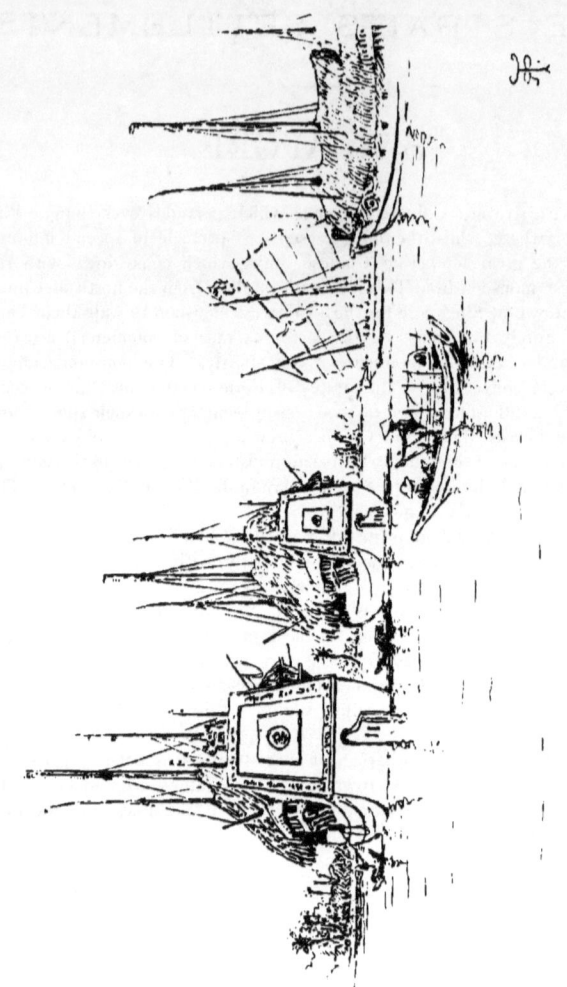

TIEN-SIEN JUNKS.

so that it was secured just at the right time. His name is coupled with a very beautiful pitcher plant, *Nepenthes Rafflesiansis*, from Borneo, and other botanical discoveries, one of which was an enormous vine growth from the same country.

Another Chinese characteristic very prominent are the small rowing boats, partially covered. These are generally known as "sampans," very light to pull and handle. They are frequently rowed by women, sometimes a mother with her picaninny on her back plying for hire at the landing places. Many of these celestials form quite a water population, although nothing to compare with such cities as Canton, where half the inhabitants are like water fowl.

THE STRAITS SETTLEMENTS.

SINGAPORE KOLEHS.

SAILING BOATS.—" Kolehs," " Koleh Panjail " Malay name. These fishing boats are full of character, very long and narrow, rigged with a large sprit-sail and jib or staysail, and frequently a small mizen is set with a leg-of-mutton or jib head ; the bow comes up to a heavy head with a corresponding stern post. The European fashion of regattas is warmly taken up wherever Englishmen go, and as a Crown colony Singapore must have a regatta, and that is the time to see " kolehs " at their best.

The English in their love of water and anything in the way of water sports not only encourage their own idea of what boats should be, but do all in their power to mature the native ideas and models, by giving prizes to the local craft, an encouragement of which the Malays very readily avail themselves, whilst they are quick in taking up any improvement they see either in handling or tuning up a boat for racing purposes. Probably, for instance, they have seen some Englishman in his one rater at Singapore leaning over on the weather side with his feet under the " stringer " and his body over the gunwale to windward, as outside ballast ; they adopt it at once, with this difference, that putting their feet on the gunwale and hanging on to the runners or shrouds the whole weight of the body becomes outside ballast to windward as shown in the illustration. How quickly fashions spread. In America the crew will lie out on boards ; the "stringer" method to hold and support the legs comes from Sydney, and the Bourne End week in England of small raters affords many details of the same principle applied to obtain outside weather ballast.

This is not the only symptom of native teachableness. He likes plenty of canvas, and garbs his pet to profusion. He loves the rush of waters with a roaring wake, with spray well over the bow, and he gets it ; and if they do turn turtle, he can swim, and he likes it, being fairly amphibious and

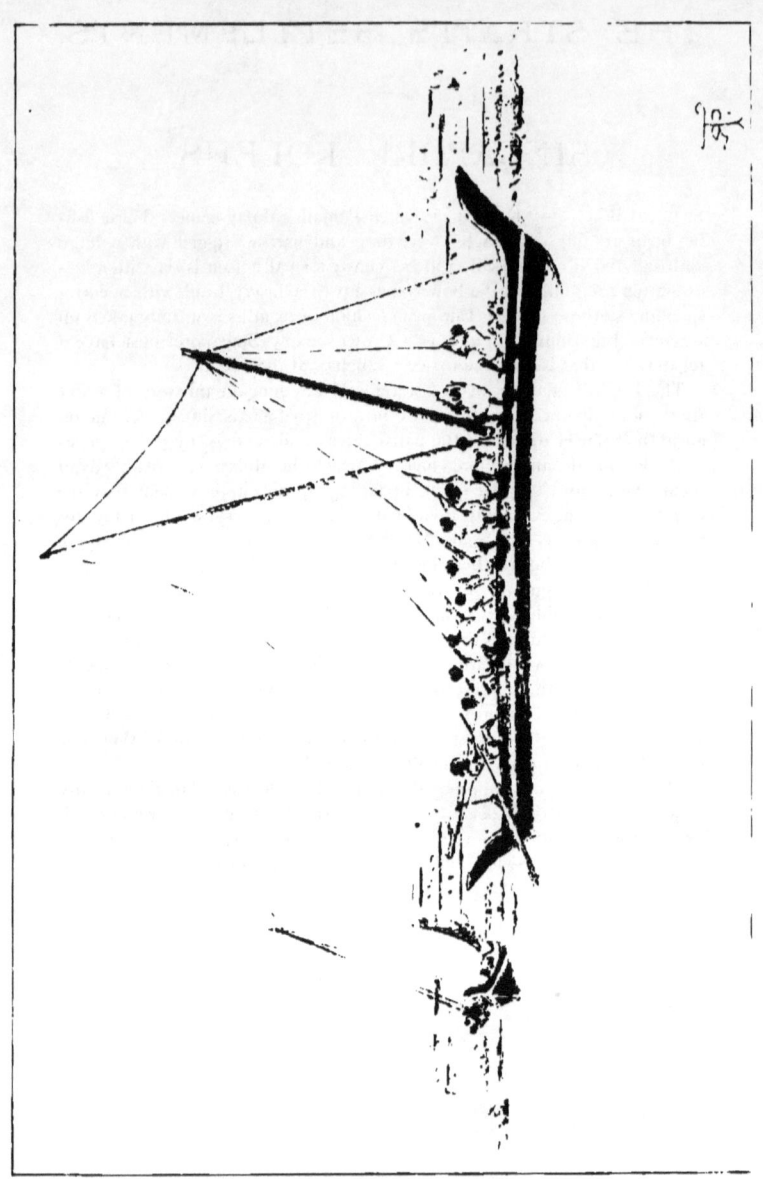

thoroughly game. All this does good; it shows the natives the English character in a sympathetic phase of kindliness and wholesome fraternity.

When racing these boats carry about fourteen hands, and are now so advanced in their suits of canvas that they carry huge spinnakers. They are very proud of having their own racing colours flying at the end of the sprit; it is a small thing, but encourages self-respect amongst them. The English encourage sport in a wide sense, not confining the racing to the Malays. There are so many Chinese in the colony that they must not be forgotten, as the Chinese are given to sailing. Prizes are given to "sampans" or rowing boats, and this notice of them is highly appreciated, creating a vast amount of good feeling towards the "outer barbarian" from the heathen Chinee.

JAVA.

PEKALONGAN FISHING BOAT.

EVERYTHING in Java seems interesting, even to the moderately observant eye; the contrast of the invading Dutch to the natives is so pronounced in every way. The Malay with bright colours, so opposite to the sombre, almost funereal black cloth of the Hollander, who still continues to wear the tall chimney-pot hat of his native land, and never omits to take his " pite " or schnapps in the most orthodox manner. The bright and gaily coloured sarongs worn by the women, picturesque with dark hair beautifully dressed, and their graceful figures. Then the scenery is grand and impressive, and craters in the mountain range fume from time to time, many of them visible from any eminence; for Java contained in 1887 twenty-one live volcanoes.

The Pekalongan fishing boat suggests a straight lineage from the old Roman galley, with high prow painted and the quaint stern with a rudder oar. They are about 48 ft. in length, with a narrow long sail with a very high peak to it, a crew some fourteen in all, whilst elaborately carved upright standards support the odd gear composed of spare bamboos, water jars, chatties, rugs, sarongs. Above this again run several bamboos to enable the skipper to descry any signs of fish, at the same time taking a bird's eye view of his crew and how they are working. This is very important, as the Malay displays few traits of energy. The sail is made of a coarse fibre and grown for this work particularly; the whole sail is rolled up in a most simple way.

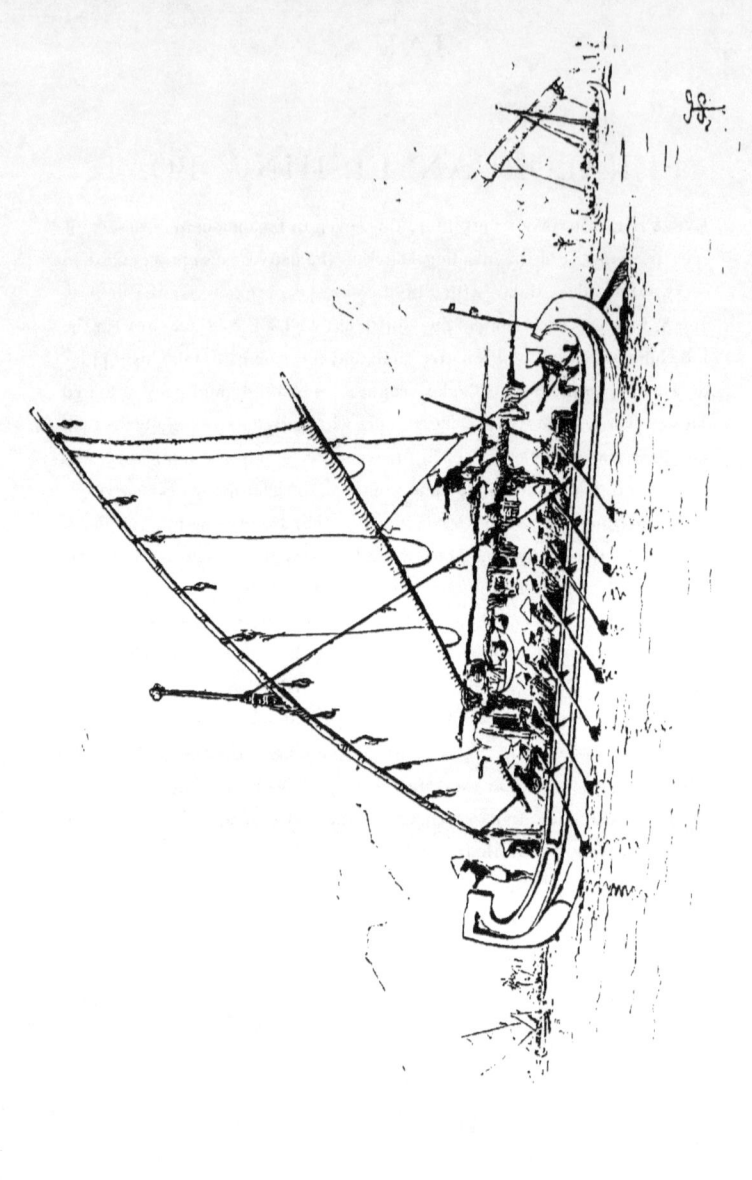

There are a number of sharks about this part, and yet a native generally swims round the boat. The only way that the natives account for his safety is that the splashing of seven paddles on either side frightens them. Some of the sails have broad terra-cotta coloured stripes, which are very effective. The rich coloured garments hanging from the superstructure add very much to the pictorial beauty of the scene.

JAVA.

PROBOLINGO FISHING BOAT.

The Probolingo boats of this class carry the native name of "sukung," and are in the hull much like those of the Sulu Archipelago up to the north, whilst the sail is quite different to those at Pekalongan, which are of thicker fibre and rolled up when furled, whereas this description of craft is more of the Fiji type, with the mast very differently placed, and much lighter in substance, the lower end of the yard going into a bucket forward and, resting in that, takes the weight off the mast. Another striking feature is the different arrangement of the outrigger supports, the one forward being low down and that aft curving up pronouncedly, to allow the wash to pass under freely when the vessel is at her high speed. This is the same on both sides, as this boat is a double outrigger. The ornamentation along the gunwale gives a very picturesque appearance, and the anchor, Heathen Chinee pattern, is very eastern.

Coming away from Celebes to visit Java, the island of Madoera is left on the starboard hand to arrive at Soerabaje. So travelling we pass some fishing craft which have come out of the bight from Probolingo, on the north side of the island and near the eastern extremity. This is the grandest approach to Java, and the two live volcanoes, "Semeroe," 3,670 ft., and "Bromo," 2,100 ft., partly enveloped in cloud vapour and smoke gradually loom and finally tower over us. This is in reality a Terra del Fuego, with nineteen live volcanoes in the island. With so many vents for volcanic fury it seems extraordinary that such a submarine outburst should have occurred at Krakatoa in the Straits of Sunma in 1883. None of the nineteen were in eruption when we were there, only fuming with a suggestion that they had "banked" fires. When visiting the celebrated botanical gardens at Buitenzorg, famed for its epidendrons amongst other wonders, we frequently looked up at the volcano "Salak" just

PROBOLINGO FISHING BOAT.

over our heads, as we heard during the morning that he had been rather restless for the last few days, and the temperature of the water in the wells had risen.

The white hats of the crew were very like Chinese head protectors. The Chinese coolies are found pretty well everywhere, especially in recently developed countries, but as a sea-going people they have done nothing to be compared with roving Malays and pirates of that ilk. Perhaps they would object to the title of pirates ; but armed yachtsmen who cruise about helping themselves to anything they may fancy, on sea or shore, such were and still are the sea gipsies or Bajaus of North-East Borneo and the Sulu Archipelago.

CELEBES.

MACASSAR CRAFT.

These vessels should be included in the ark or house-boat class, as we live in an age of classification. Celebes runs from the Equator 0°, in a long slip of an island down to 5° south, lying to the eastward of the lower part of Borneo, so that it is rather out of the way and not much frequented by Europeans, save a few Dutchmen who come up from Java.

The craft here are the most villagey looking vessels we know; it would have been very interesting to have gone over the establishment to see how they were arranged. The large parallelogrammic sail with the wide band of colour running through it is quite Malay in form and character, so also the outside rudder and inverted beak stern; the Derrick masts and heavy mast-head belong to the same school. The houses represent the local peculiarity, and very odd they are, the only reason one can give to account for all the thatching resorted to is that in these equatorial latitudes the smaller boats adopted the same protection against the sun's perpendicular rays, and as it is so successful in the smaller essays the Celebes people thought they would show the world what they could do in their own waters.

The boat on the right in this illustration is a two-master with Probolingo

MACASSAR CRAFT, CELEBES.

sails going before the wind goosewinged : she too has a thatched roof in a more moderate degree. The rig is very picturesque, and much more pleasing to the eye than the Celebes sail rolled up in the vessel in the centre. Quaint as they appear, they were carefully drawn and are faithful to the originals. The heaviness of the hulls is admirably relieved by the ornamentation round the gunwale, which is a Mohammedan green pattern on a white ground, the Malays being mostly Moslems.

BORNEO.

PIRATE CRAFT.

INDIVIDUAL energy and foresight have often sprung a mine of wealth in starting the small end of the commercial wedge for the ultimate benefit of the Mother Country. A prominent case is that of Rajah Brooke of Sarawak. Borneo is an immense island, next in size to Australia, and now held by the Dutch in the lower half and by the English in the upper and better half. Pirates infested the whole coast, particularly on the Eastern side, and inland the Dyaks were equally troublesome. Sir James Brooke formed a settlement at Sarawak, which is really difficult of access, up a very narrow river, the channel of which is indicated by finger boards, "Keep close to right bank," &c., &c., and in 1841 he was appointed Rajah of Sarawak.

In 1843 Captain H. Keppel was on the coast and tackled the pirates to his heart's content and their great discomfort, but in fact they are not yet cleared out. Borneo, at that time, 1844, was little known in this country, in fact hardly heard of. One morning the master of our class at school alarmed us by ordering couplets to be written by every boy present "on Borneo." Some of us wondered who it was, where it was, and when it was. One lad, however, was up to date, and his stanza has frequently recurred to my mind ever since. It ran thus:—

"Rajah Brooke the pirate took
  In the war of Borneo,
And Captain Keppel wrote a book
  All about that war, ye know."

The Dyaks are great head hunters, a proclivity still carried on in the interior. Rajah Brooke got them well in hand, and now the comparatively

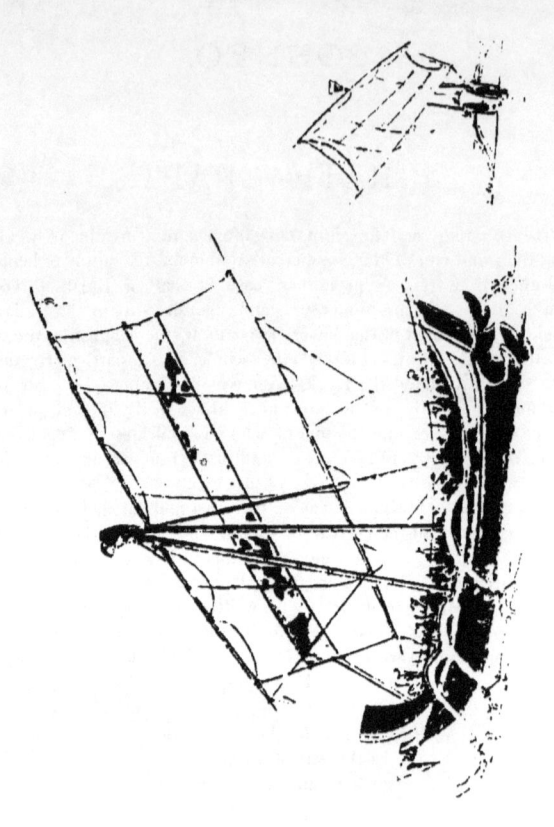

gentle Dyak uses his "Eilean Pareng" for more domestic purposes than the decapitation of his neighbours or enemies. The weapon still remains general amongst them; the blade is about 22 in. long, 1½ in. wide at the end, and only ¾ in. at the handle, which is made of Sambur deer horn, elaborately carved and ornamented, as well as the scabbard, with tufts of black and red hair.

The pirate craft are very narrow, with two large outriggers, so that when seen stem on they have the appearance of vast water spiders. The huge sail is made of fibre; to furl it it is rolled up; round the bulwarks are numerous bamboos to form a kind of balustrade instead of a life-line. The pirates used to be armed with heavy "parengs," interspersed with a great variety of bills and catchpoles, instruments shown by the warders in the Tower of London. The accommodation on board is very much limited, in fact hardly required in such a lovely climate as lat. 5° N.

The north part of this vast island is known as British North Borneo, now rapidly developing under a royal charter, with Sandaken for its capital, under the Protectorate of Great Britain. This was obtained in 1888. The natives are indolent, but the proximity of Chinese supply many who are too glad to settle down under peaceful English rule and grow vegetables, and John Chinaman does that admirably anywhere, wherever he may be.

BORNEO.

SULU CRAFT AT SANDAKAU.

THIS schooner-rigged craft was rather a surprise when she loomed in the distance, heading for Sandakau Bay and Harbour. When she brought up she presented a very home-made but foreign appearance, for her masts were comparatively untrimmed sticks with bowsprit *en suite*. She was carrying Mahommedans on a pilgrimage to Mecca, with the ladies in the thatched house midships; poor things, would they ever get there? did they ever get there? Deponent sayeth not.

She is not a bad craft in design, and has lines very like an Arab dhow, which can go anywhere, with the Indian Ocean for its natural *habitat*, with Bombay at one end and the Red Sea and Berbera for the other. Were they converted Sea Bajaus, determined to atone for all their past sins by this little yachting expedition across the Indian Ocean? They ought to be all right up to Acheen Head, when, if the pirates of that lively locality did not stop them, they would have then to face the dangers of the deep. That is not all; when they arrive at the sacred object of that

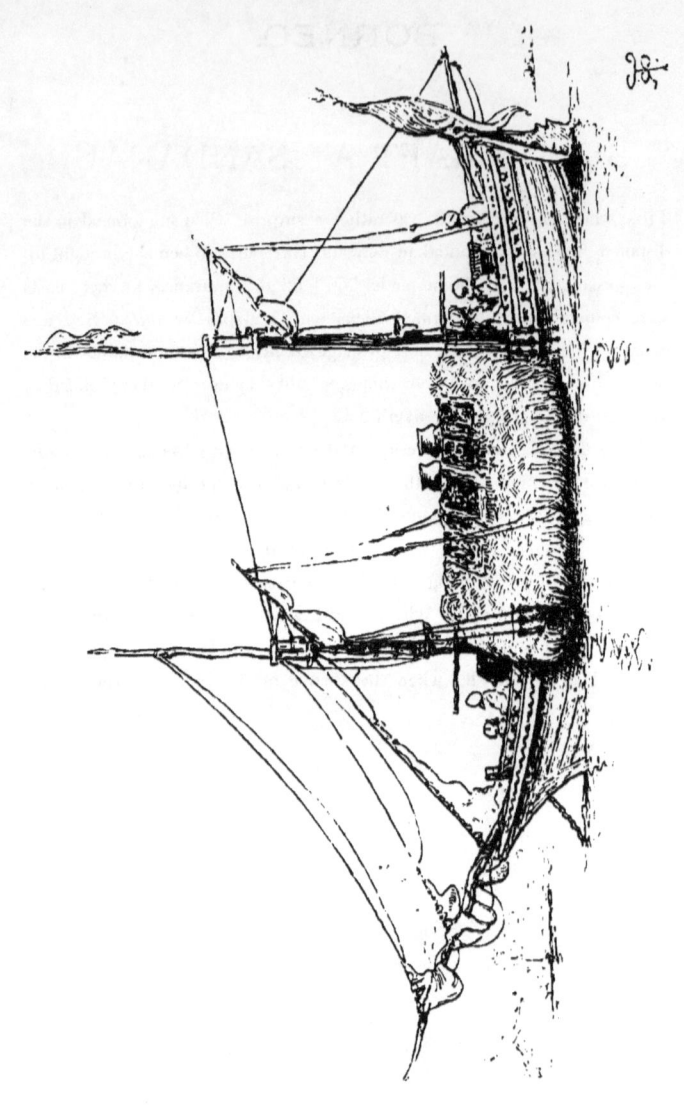

pilgrimage the great event of their lives is not completed—there is the return.

Fanaticism is a powerful master, and there is something very grand in their faith that "Allah is almighty, all graciousness." So they will, with all patience and resignation, start back with bright hopes, having a full conviction that they have only fulfilled what they conceived to be their religious duty; and duty is a better master than fanaticism.

CHINA.

CHINESE PIRATE JUNK.

THE Chinese junks in their ponderous class, the Tien-sien annual traders, have been already shown and referred to at Singapore. This is one of a very different class, and for a less pacific purpose. Built for speed if required, it resembles the fishing craft type seen off Hong Kong when making for the Lymoon Channel.

As we came up from Java to the Straits of Banka under the lee of the island we saw an English barque becalmed, at the same time we saw two pirate junks bound on visiting her, and getting out their long sweeps after we had passed them. Being on board a foreign mail boat bound for Singapore, we could do nothing. The captain, when we noticed the incident, only remarked that "those junks do very good business always about here." Of course at the north point of Sumatra the pirates are their friends, and the Dutch Government have a small man-of-war frequently cruising about there to protect any strangers coming to or passing that part.

These two junks were crowded with men, and although everything in the way of armament was secreted there is no doubt but that they had plenty on board, besides which every Chinaman would have in this case his dagger fan. The Chinese carry their fans down at the back in the nape of the neck, so that they are entirely hidden. When, therefore, you see a Chinaman pull out rather a longer fan than the usual size, you may be sure

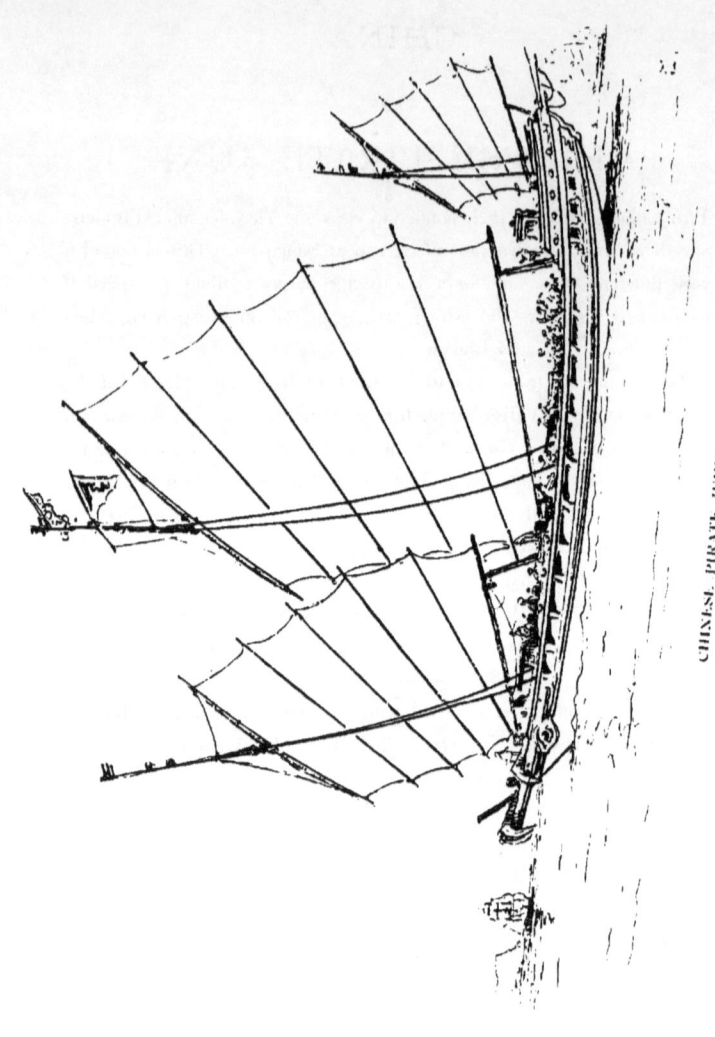

CHINESE PIRATE JUNK.
Off Banka Islands, Sumatra.

that it is a dagger fan with a very nasty blade inside. Nefarious as is the life of these fellows, the joss-house on the poop is always made very prominent, and the whole appointments of the ship are good. The heavy anchors carried in the bow on those strong timbers only avert the attention from the fine lines and enhance the national character of these craft, as shown when coming in a breeze through the crest of a wave. They are splendid sea boats and steer well, although their rudders have long slots in them to lighten them, as they are very large. The China coast during the monsoons is a fine school for them to learn seamanship in.

JAPAN.

JAPANESE FISHING CRAFT.

JAPAN, till lately, was a sealed country. China always resisted the outer barbarian and does so still, but not now Japan. To Nagasaki, a very small island, the Dutch traders used to be confined. Only once a year were they permitted to land, so that the Japs did not encourage foreign trade in the days of James I. In fact, so determined were they to keep to themselves that all boats and vessels were built on one model, which is seen still, and fulfils the purpose for which it was first intended — to be a coaster only, but not a sea-going craft to reach a foreign shore.

It was only in 1856 that Nagasaki and the extreme northern port of Japan Hakodadi were opened to European commerce. But since that time developments have been rapid. In 1877 an ironclad was built and launched for them in the Thames. A railway was opened in 1870. Lighthouses, a second railway, post offices, national costume doomed, religious freedom established in this land of magnificent temples, all crowned by that best of civilisers, free trade, a really open door for the good influence of other countries more advanced than themselves — all this followed. Their navy is now composed of up-to-date vessels with every modern appliance, as proved by their display against their neighbours the slow Chinese, whose lack of discipline was their ruin, and the admirable discipline of the Japs their irresistible strength. Even their mercy during the war astonished their enemies, who all expected to be murdered when taken, instead of which the Japs, who are never cruel, treated with every consideration all their prisoners.

Meeting the Japanese Minister of Marine at the Mayor's banquet, at Liverpool, after inspecting H.M. torpedo catcher "Rattlesnake," our conversation turned to the vast seaboard of Japan. This afforded a good

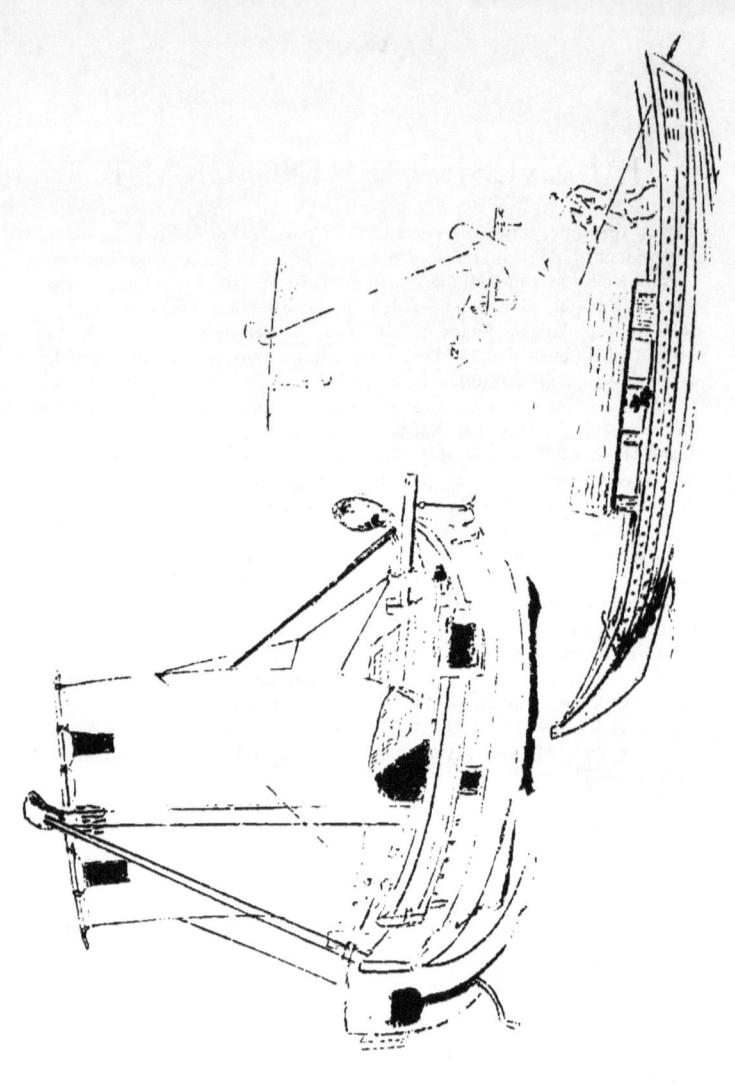

opportunity to recommend our admirable system of lifeboats all round our own coasts. The offer to supply his Excellency with details from our National Lifeboat Institution was readily accepted, and just lately some Japanese naval officers who were visiting Thorneycroft's works at Chiswick, to inspect some torpedo catchers in course of construction for their Government, informed me that several lifeboat stations have been successfully established and have done much good.

There is one class of fishing which is very curious, to our minds certainly, and we, coming upon it unexpectedly, were thoroughly surprised. Who would expect to see whales taken in nets? Still, having seen it we believe it, and the Japanese officers confirmed it as being still in vogue. The mesh of the net is about two feet or more of stout rope. No little dexterity is required to get into the net these monsters of the deep ; they are, however, to use a yachting expression, not sixty footers when once netted. The fishers roll them round and round until they are almost dead when brought alongside. The next function is to tow the prize home in its net shroud.

The fisher boats form a very imposing sight as they come out of Yokohama, in number about two hundred, each sail marked with some black hieroglyphic with fusihama, their sacred mountain coming in the background as naturally as if the boats were on a Japanese tea tray. Surely this model will soon be outclassed ; they hardly harmonise with the modern war craft now rapidly imported. Their tonnage is about 100 tons.

Length, 84 ft. Beam, 24 ft. Depth, 6 ft. to 7 ft. What a contrast to the Prince of Wales' racing cutter " Britannia," she being all below, and the Jap all above the water line. It is worth while to repeat the figures of these two crafts :—

	THE ENGLISH YACHT.	JAPANESE VESSEL.
L. Water line	87·8 ft.	... 84 ft.
Beam	... 23·66 ft.	... 24 ft.
Draught	... 15 ft.	6 ft. to 8 ft.
Sail area	10,328 square ft.	Probably 2,000 square ft.

The excellence and thoroughness of all Japanese manufacture is quite maintained in the workmanship of the boat-builders. All their joinery is so accurate, that we tremble lest in competition they should lower their standard of quality, which is a strong national feature. Much of this excellency of finish is due to the daimios or feudal lords, who strove for quality from their artificers.

BRAZIL.

BAHIA RIVER CRAFT.

BAHIA is a lovely spot in a delightful climate about lat. 13 S. Entering a fine bay, a beautiful view opens up; the whole well-known Reconcava of Bahia lies before us, and on the right, on a high cliff, is built the bright looking town of Bahia, where Brazilian hospitality awaits every genial visitor. The whole country here is rich in production of tobacco, sugar, and Brazil nuts. Off Para the numerous tributary rivers offer great facility of communication by water conveyance—a system already yielding to steam and railways which bring down in profusion every variety of tropical produce, pine-apples, bread-fruit, bananas, tapioca, yams, sago, coffee, and many more beside. The long name for this interesting place is Bahia dos Todos os Santos; Anglice, the Bay of All Saints. The inhabitants are certainly furiously enthusiastic, with the ringing of bells, endless services, continuous firing of rockets in the daytime to announce the elevation of the Host; squibs, crackers, in honour and respect for priests and nuns. Then the market is quite a feature, the gaily ribboned negresses from the sugar plantations, the costumes of the people from the country, half Portuguese, and the rest Indian, in ponchos, the most comfortable of garments, some from Feira Santos Anna, like Chilian Huassos, with heavy silver spurs and brown leather hats and coats—these are the daring horsemen of the district. It was a wonderful sight altogether, particularly the

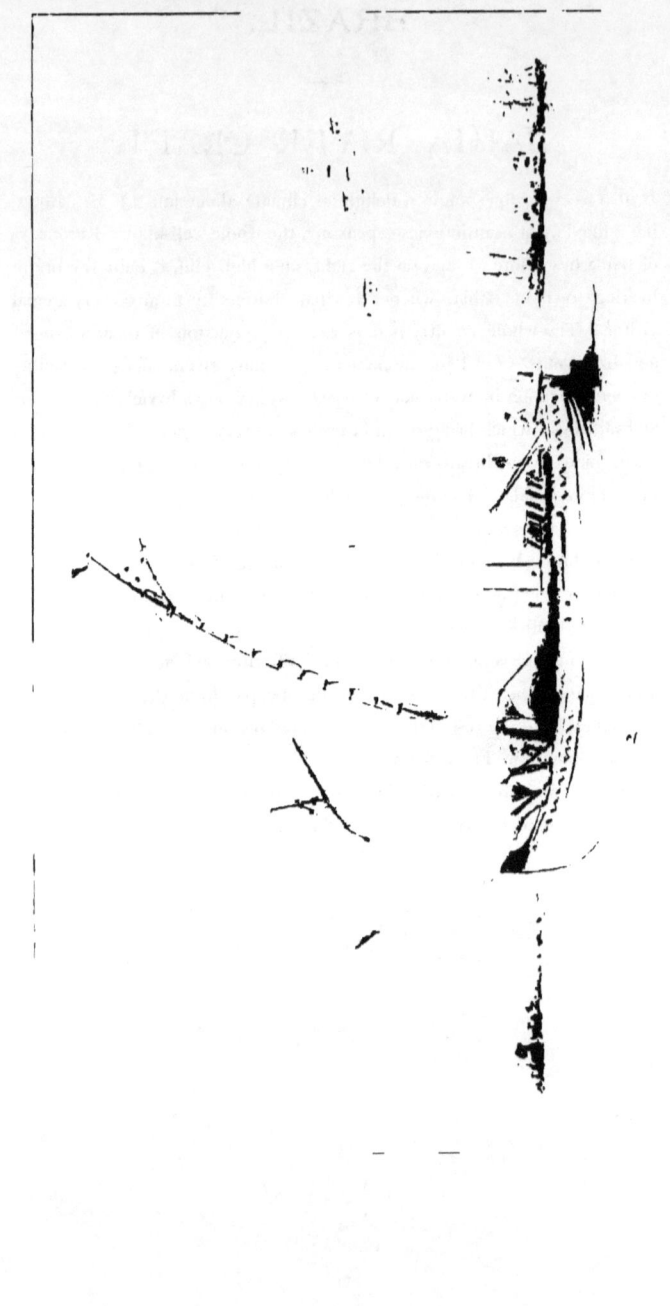

jubilant negresses in a blaze of bright coloured petticoats and such bedecked bonnets as they returned from Mass.

The tributary rivers have made Bahia a large central station of commerce, and for that reason the sailing craft, of which but few remain, should be carefully recorded. It will be remarked that there is evidently a palpable impress of Portuguese character: in fact, a distant relation of the hay boat on the Tagus, ere long to give way to river steamers and local "tramps," the name we have for steam coasting cargo boats. The canvas of these vessels is very limited, and the curious little foremast in the bow seems hardly more workmanlike than a staysail. But so it has been handed down to them and faithfully adhered to, doing good work in its day, which will have been rather a long one ere it shall be totally discarded.

CHILI.

THE BOLSA OR SKIN BOAT AT COQUIMBO.

THE Bay of Coquimbo in Chili, above Valparaiso, is the *habitat* of this particular kind of bullock-skin raft, for it cannot be dignified by the name of boat, although it carries canvas, yet it does good service to the natives who have no boats. The Chilians are not aquatic in any way. Horses, ponchos, good cuchillios, horse furniture. large wooden richly carved stirrups to protect the boots going through the low scrub with which Chili abounds: these are more like the Penates of the Chilian than boats or sea life.

It is remarkable that in going all along the Chilian and west coast of South America there is no local kind of rig or craft to be seen, and this not for want of a lead. For instance, Coquimbo is rather a favourite harbour, where British men-of-war are frequently seen. Then during the Peruvian and Chilian war boats of all kinds were constantly cruising and sailing about from English, French, German, Italian, Russian, Spanish men-of-war which were lying at Callao Bay for a length of time.

The simple construction of this bolsa is seen at once. It is formed by two bullock skins inflated, lashed together with a kind of platform, a very simple superstructure for the voyager to be seated on. A small sail wafts him along when he gets a fair wind, which is most desirable, for with a

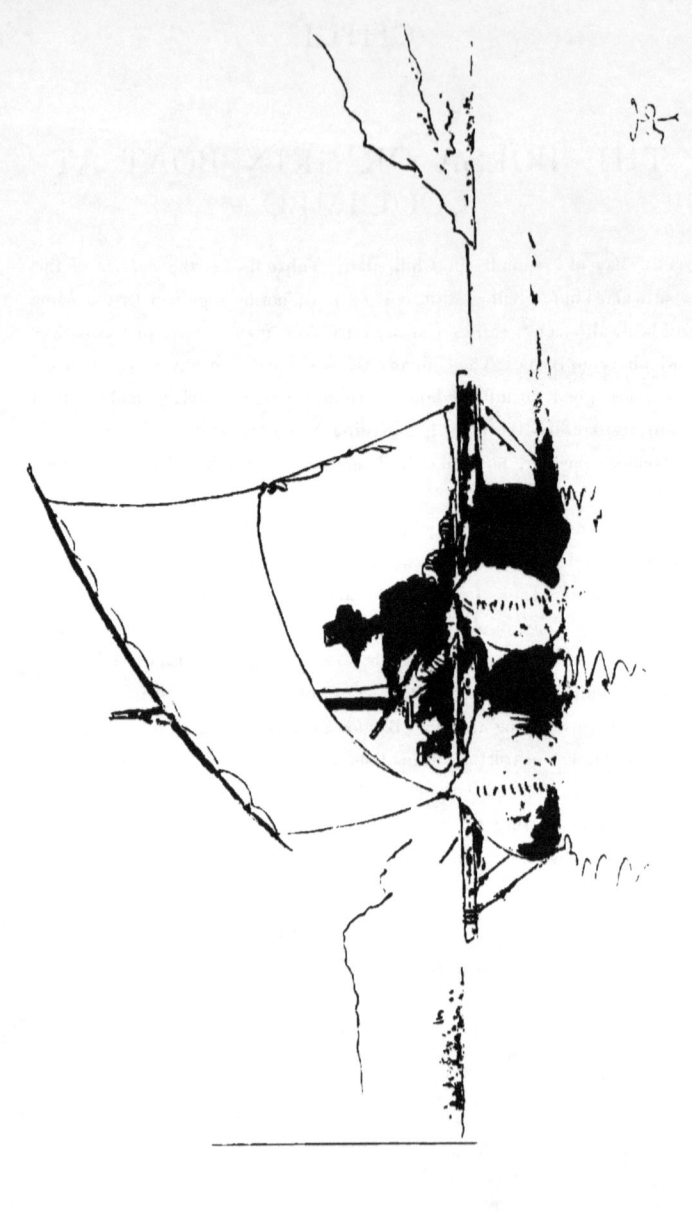

head wind she would sag to leeward, like a Portuguese man-of-war or a haystack, in spite of paddles or anything else. The Portuguese man-of-war, or madusa, has wonderful power below her water-line, whilst the bolsa is quite on the surface; and as she has to be beached after her little trips, a lead keel would be rather a superfluity. They might try a centre-board between the two skins, but they prefer to live and die simple Coquimbo bolsas. One step towards improvement would destroy the individuality of what now stands alone to meet the simple wants and ideas of the natives in that locality.

FIJI.

THE LEVUKA.

Fiji is a word that recalls at once marvellous stories of South Sea adventure, of pagan rites, of sacrificial altars composed of huge blocks of tufa, with a few skulls lying about, old cocoa-nut hammocks slung from forked poles, with a taboo cocoa-nut pendant, a warning to strangers, should any visit the sacred spot. Each plaited hammock contains a body: it is the mode of burial, if that term may be applied in this case of *al fresco* cemeteries. The natives are most superstitious, having a great objection to going out after dark. The most convenient and very best time therefore, to visit such an interesting locality is by moonlight alone. Step softly, and should you pick up a skull, do not be surprised if a harmless lizard runs out of it; it is only anxious to escape from unwarrantable intrusion.

The King, Thakombau (spelt "Cakobau), was an imposing figure, wrapped in tapa of fine quality. Over eighty years of age, he stood six feet two inches, dignified in the extreme, whilst his son "Ratu" (Tim), of the same height and general appearance, stood by him. He has now passed away, and the royal gift of a human meat-dish is greatly treasured by me, especially as the king's favourite carver was presented to us, instead of our being presented to him. Ratu Ambarosa, the king's nephew, told us that the carver's official duties ceased in 1876. but from old association they retained the stone arrangement where the long pig was cooked, and he showed it to us with considerable zest, as he described the details of the old ceremonies. King Thakombau assured us that he was very glad to be under "Marama" (Queen Victoria), but it disturbed all his good old-fashioned habits. Judging from the stately appearance of the royal father and his two sons, the diet of former days had agreed with them.

The natives are a very fine race, their precision of drill admirable, as shown in their war dances, or "mekimekis." of which we saw many under the most favourable circumstances, having arrived just before the Flying Squadron, in September, 1881. War canoes had rendezvoused there from all the surrounding islands. *Fêtes* were prepared, and a royal "angona," or kava festival. It was really a revival of the old habits, customs, and

ceremonies, without carniverous luxuries, of bygone days. Special efforts were made, even by the missionaries, as the squadron brought " Marama's " two grandsons, who, though only "middies" on board H.M.S. "Bacchante," were really the H.R.H. Prince Albert Victor and his brother, Prince George.

The squadron consisted of H.M.S. "Inconstant," flagship of Admiral the Earl of Clanwilliam ; H.M.S. "Tourmaline," H.M.S. "Bacchante," with the princes on board ; H.M.S. "Cleopatra," and H.M.S. "Carysfort." It was a grand sight as they approached under canvas, taking it in as they approached, finally coming in under easy steam. King Thakombau went out in his double canoe beyond the reef to welcome them. He was accompanied by his two sons, and we were told that the four flags indicated that his Majesty had his four wives on board his double-bodied canoe. This detail we do not vouch for, as it might have emanated from a reporter for the Levuka society paper, so soon do converted savages take on the evils of what we call civilisation.

The canoes here are naturally wonderfully handled, and we had a delightful cruise with Ratu Ambarosa. We went out to pick up crab pots, which was a surprising performance, for after just looking round to take his bearings, over he went, and came up with the crab pot ; Ratu, radiant like bright copper in the sunshine, with huge head of hair of golden colour, dripping in cascades on to his shoulders. The Somalis of North Africa have strong heads of hair, but nothing to a Fiji native. To produce the fashionable old gold colour, "chinam," or calcined coral, is applied for a week.

THE ANTIPODES.

A CANOE OF THE ABORIGINES.

So many now run to and fro, and knowledge has been so much increased by the facility of communication between the north and south, east and west, that we cannot but be convinced that our globe is not so immense as we thought it was when it took in many cases six months for a letter to reach its destination; say from India to England. What a change from the beginning of the present century to the present day, especially in rapid water conveyances. The sketch shown here in conclusion gives an idea of what Australia was in 1801, when Port Jackson had only canoes manned by the aborigines. It is one of a series of drawings taken by William Westall, A.R.A., landscape painter to the celebrated expedition of discovery and survey on the coast of Australia, commanded by Captain M. Flinders, of H.M.S. "Investigator," in the years 1801, 1802, 1803.

The whole collection is of the greatest historical interest, comprising the entire series of sketches made by Westall during the expedition. Before he accepted the appointment he stipulated that his original drawings should be returned to him after the requirements of the Admiralty had been fulfilled. The Admiralty returned them accordingly, and they have been in the possession of the family up to the time of their acquirement by the Royal Colonial Institute in Northumberland Avenue, who are to be

A CANOE OF THE ABORIGINES.

heartily congratulated on having become possessed of such a valuable historical colonial treasure, which will in their hands be safely preserved and carefully nurtured.

The canoe shown here is one of the Murray Isles (lat. 10° S.) craft. The sketch was made when the canoes came alongside H.M.S. "Investigator," offering cocoa-nuts and bows for barter, and is reproduced by the kind permission of the Council of the Institute.

The Gresham Press:
UNWIN BROTHERS,
WOKING AND LONDON

www.ingramcontent.com/pod-product-compliance
Lightning Source LLC
Chambersburg PA
CBHW031815230426
43669CB00009B/1153